JEANS AND A T-SHIRT

Fun and Fabulous Upcycling Projects for Denim and More

Niki Meiners

STACKPOLE
BOOKS

Guilford, Connecticut

Stackpole Books
An imprint of The Rowman & Littlefield Publishing Group, Inc.
4501 Forbes Blvd., Ste. 200
Lanham, MD 20706
www.rowman.com

Distributed by
NATIONAL BOOK NETWORK
800-462-6420

British Library Cataloguing in Publication Information Available

Library of Congress Cataloging-in-Publication Data
ISBN 978-0-8117-1802-8 (paperback)
ISBN 978-0-8117-6753-8 (e-book)

♾™ The paper used in this publication meets the minimum requirements of
American National Standard for Information Sciences—Permanence of Paper
for Printed Library Materials, ANSI/NISO Z39.48-1992.

Printed in the United States of America

Dedication

This book would not have been possible without the encouragement of my crafty friends Carla, Jen, Keri, and Melony; my sewing mentors, Beth and Bethany; and my mother, Anna. I am also eternally grateful to my husband, Gary, and my kids, Maxx and Gigi, for their never-ending support of my crazy ideas.

Contents

PROJECTS

Introduction

It is easy to remake everyday clothing you already have on hand into sophisticated home decor and handmade gifts. All it takes is a little ingenuity and basic sewing skills. With this book as your guide, you can create extraordinary one-of-a kind handmade gifts and decorative accents by recycling everyday clothing such as jeans and T-shirts. Each denim or T-shirt project is fun to make and even more fun to give as a gift! Just follow the simple instructions to make gifts and home decor that are both budget-friendly and eco-conscious.

Let's get started!

My Favorite Tools and Materials

There are many tools and materials that I reach for again and again in my studio, and these are ones that are used in many of the projects in this book. You don't need to have all of these on hand, but they are what I consider essentials for my crafting. Each project includes a list of the specific tools and materials used in the project; refer to that list before you begin a project to make sure you have what you need. Here are my must-haves:

- 8-inch fabric scissors
- 4-inch fabric scissors
- Sewing machine
- Sewing machine needles for denim (16/100)
- Jean-A-Ma-Jig
- Needles: upholstery, assorted craft
- Thread: heavy duty, denim, waxed
- Straight pins
- Seam ripper
- Cover button kit
- Fiberfill
- Fusible fleece
- Interlining
- Poly-Pellets (weighted stuffing material)
- Pillow forms
- Iron-on letters
- Die-cut machine and dies
- Stencils
- Fabric paint
- Paintbrushes
- Fabric glue
- Rotary cutter and mat
- Ruler

I am often asked what specific products I use, so I list those here for your reference, but they are by no means the only brands available. I use these brands because they are reliable and easy to find in most big box stores and online. Find what you like and what fits in your budget and use it. You don't have to break the bank to make great things.

- **Westcott:** ExtremEdge 8" Bent Adjustable Tension Titanium Bonded Scissors, 4" Titanium Bonded Detail Cut Sewing Scissors
- **Coats and Clark:** Dual Duty XP Thread—Denim or Heavy Weight Thread
- **Prym Dritz:** Jean-A-Ma-Jig, Denim/Jeans Machine Needles 16/100, Straight Pins, Seam Fix Seam Ripper, Craft Cover Button Kit, Upholstery Needle, Waxed Thread, 25-Piece Assorted Craft Needles, Grommet Pliers
- **Fairfield Processing Corporation:** Poly-Fil Fiberfill, Smooth Fusible Fleece, Stick Interlining, Poly-Pellets, Biggie Bean Bag Filler, Crafter's Choice Pillow Forms
- **Joy:** Iron-on Letters
- **Sizzix:** Big Shot Pro, Big Shot, Baby Bib die (item #660924), Bigz Heart die (item #660789), Star die (item #A10181), Tag die (item #660280)
- **DecoArt:** Stencils, Acrylic Paint, Paintbrushes
- **Beacon Adhesives:** Fabri-Tac Permanent Stiffen Stuff Adhesive
- **Omnigrid:** Rotary cutter, cutting mat, rulers in different shapes and sizes. *A rotary cutter is optional but very helpful for working with denim and T-shirt material.*

Some of the projects in this book use clasps or buckles, such as slide adjusters, parachute buckles, D-rings, and swivel hooks.

Cover buttons allow you to make buttons from fabric to coordinate with any project.

Grommet pliers are used to set decorative stud embellishments.

You will want a good pair of scissors, strong denim needles, and thread. Cording and a rotary cutter may come in handy, too.

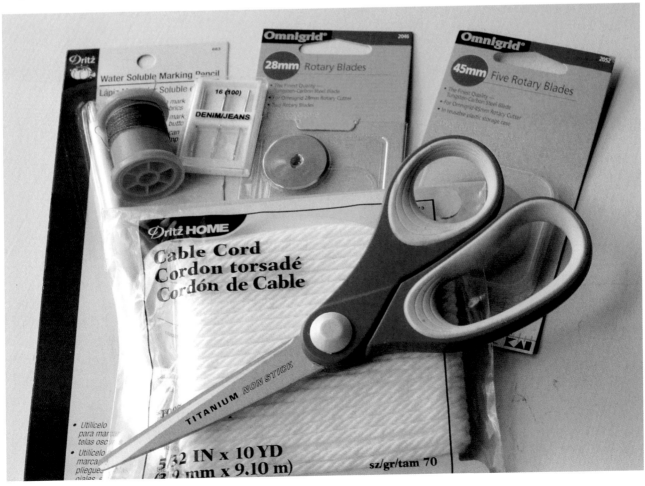

A die-cutter like the Sizzix Big Shot can cut pieces of fabric in nice, even, identical shapes.

MY SEWING MACHINES

One question I hear often is, "What type of sewing machine do you use?" For the projects in this book, I used two machines: a Singer and a Janome. My tiny little workhorse that I take on the road is an inexpensive Singer. I think it was about $130 from an end cap at Costco. My other machine is a high-end Janome 9900 that does sewing, quilting, and embroidery. I love both machines equally. You don't need to have an expensive machine to make beautiful projects. My Janome does beautiful embroidery that has allowed me to expand what I can do in this area, but you can also hand-embroider any of these designs.

My advice is to buy the best machine that fits your budget and your needs, and then *read your manual* and *learn how to take care of the machine*, and it will last a long time no matter the price. When I first started sewing, I broke three machines beyond repair because I did not know how to use them or properly maintain them, but all the information I needed on how to take care of them was in the manuals. If you are not comfortable servicing your machine, ask for help or take it to a sewing center. If you treat it well, it can last a long time.

Deconstructing Jeans

'm often asked, "How do I take apart a pair of jeans?" My answer is that it depends on your needs. Deconstructing denim can be done in a variety of ways depending on your end use. Some pants I want to use purely for their pockets, and others I want for their fabric. If you are deconstructing for later use and want to save every single piece of the jeans, there is a method to take them apart, which I will also discuss.

For projects like the dog leash and the coiled trivet shown on pages 70 and 66, I wanted just the outer seams. My husband's pants are extra long, as he is 6 feet 5 inches tall, so I used his jeans for these projects. I used my heavy-duty scissors to cut along the seam from the bottom to the waistband, and then saved the rest of the denim for later use.

If I just want the pockets, I cut the legs off an inch or two from the base of the pocket on both legs. Then I cut off the sides at the side seam and the top just under the waistband. The waistband, front pockets, belt loops, and zipper are left. You can continue to disassemble the remaining pieces and store them in zip-top bags for later use, or you can store them as is and take apart when needed. I use both methods.

When fabric for a project is the main goal or I'm not sure yet what the end use will be, I deconstruct with the aim of keeping every usable piece of fabric. I use the seam ripper to remove the stitches, starting at the bottom hem, then the outer seam, leaving the inner seam intact. You can decide later if the inner seam will be used. Pockets are removed via seam ripper and stacked and stored for later use. The belt loops and waistband are removed with the seam ripper too. The zipper and remaining seams are cut with scissors.

For some projects, such as the dog leash, you will use just the seams.

Cut an inch or two under the pockets if you want just the pockets for a project.

Cut as close to the seam thread as you can, or use a seam ripper to salvage even more fabric.

This type of seam ripper also pulls out the pieces of thread as you work.

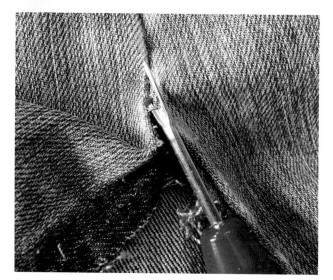

The seam ripper is the tool of choice for taking out threads along the cuff and seams

Projects

Pencil or Make-up Case

When you personalize a gift, it makes the recipient feel extra special. Iron-on letters make this project fast and are an easy way to personalize the project, too. Iron-on letters in a wide variety of sizes, fonts, and colors are available in the craft section of most big box stores. The lining of the pouch is made from a T-shirt, and the denim strips are left over from the large tote bag on page 10. Zippers can be purchased or reused from other garments.

MATERIALS

> Recycled denim fabric to make two 8- by 6-inch (20 by 15 cm) pieces
> Two 8- by 6-inch (20 by 15 cm) pieces of T-shirt lining fabric
> 7-inch (18 cm) zipper
> Sewing machine or needle and thread
> Pins
> Jean-A-Ma-Jig
> Scissors
> Rotary cutter, ruler, and mat (optional)
> Iron-on monogram letters
> Iron and ironing surface
> Optional: zipper foot for sewing machine

INSTRUCTIONS

1. Sew strips of denim together to form two pieces of fabric measuring 8 by 6 inches (20 by 15 cm).
2. Lay one outside piece face up. Lay the zipper face down on the edge with right sides together and pin in place.
3. Place one of your lining fabric pieces on top of that, face down. You should have the zipper sandwiched between the two pieces of fabric. Pin in place if needed.
4. Use a straight stitch to sew the layers together along the edge, going through both fabric pieces and the zipper. (Adjust the zipper pull as needed so you do not sew through it and break your needle.)
5. Fold the lining over and then around to the back, with the wrong sides of both the lining and main fabric touching.
6. Place the opposite edge of the zipper (opposite of previously sewn) face down onto the other main fabric piece, and place the other lining piece right-side down on top. Stitch down the edge, sewing through the fabric, lining, and zipper. Fold it open like the first pieces.
7. Check that the zipper is sewn to the correct sides, then fold one of the main fabric pieces over so that it's lying face down on top of the other. Repeat with the lining fabric. Pin in place.
8. Making sure to first unzip the zipper about halfway, sew all the way around the edges, leaving a small opening on the lining side for turning. Flip the case right-side out through the opening. Iron it flat, then stitch the opening closed either by hand or machine.

Note: For a flat zipper, fold the zipper toward the lining side so the bulk of the zipper is toward the lining side while you sew it together.

9. Iron on the monogram letters in the location of your choice.

Sailor Tote

large tote is perfect for the beach or pool. Make yours extra durable by using upcycled denim in different colors. Denim holds up well to wear and tear and is easy to wash. Give your oversize tote a nautical feel by accenting it with roping and an anchor embellishment. Save time by using a back pocket off the jeans for a side pocket on the tote bag. The small pocket is perfect for loose change and a set of keys.

MATERIALS

- › ²/₃ yard (61 cm) total of denim fabric in several colors
- › ²/₃ yard (61 cm) of T-shirt fabric for inner lining
- › ²/₃ yard (61 cm) of fusible fleece interfacing
- › 1¹/₂ yards (137 cm) of roping
- › 42 inches (107 cm) of denim (7 inches [18 cm] wide) for the strap
- › Jean-A-Ma-Jig
- › Scissors
- › Rotary cutter, ruler, and mat (optional)
- › Sewing machine with denim needle
- › Heavy-duty thread
- › Iron and ironing surface
- › Optional: anchor die-cut and die-cut machine, chain to attach anchor design

INSTRUCTIONS

1. Begin by planning out how you will design the fabric, and sew pieces of denim together as needed. Pant legs are perfect for striped pieces. I chose three colors and divided the colors by roping. Thick roping is not easy to work with. I plan to use smaller roping the next time I make this bag.

2. From the fabric you have sewn together, cut two 24- by 20-inch (61 by 51 cm) rectangles of both outer and inner fabric, then cut two 24- by 20-inch (61 by 51 cm) rectangles of fusible fleece interfacing. Iron the fusible fleece to the wrong side of the denim fabric, following the manufacturer's instructions, and trim off any excess fabric.

3. Form strap by cutting your fabric strips and fusible interfacing to size, approximately 21 inches (53 cm) each. Adhere interfacing to wrong side of fabric. The interfacing adds a touch of stability to the strap and a little padding too.

4. Fold the strip in half lengthwise, wrong sides together, pressing with an iron to crease. It is important to do this accurately.

5. Fold in the raw edges to meet the center crease and press with the iron.

6. Fold in half again on the original crease and make sure the edges line up perfectly. Pin in place if desired.

7. Set the sewing machine stitch length to 3–3.5. You want a nice distance for your topstitching. Stitch along the open sides ¹/₈ to ¹/₄ inch (0.3 to 0.6 cm) in and repeat for the other side. Then repeat at equidistant intervals down the center of the strap.

8. On the long side of all four bag rectangles, snip a 2- by 2-inch (5 by 5 cm) square from only the bottom corners.

9. Pin the outer fabric with right sides together and sew straight ¹/₂-inch (1.3 cm) seams along the sides and bottom of the piece.

Note: Leave the top and two snipped corners unsewn.

10. Press seams open and pinch together the gaps in the snipped corners, lining up the side and bottom seams in the center. Pin the fabric straight and sew a ¹/₂-inch (1.3 cm) seam. This step adds depth to the bag and creates a flat bottom.

11. Flip the liner right-side out and place inside the outer fabrics, right sides together. Place the denim straps approximately 4 inches (10 cm) from the side seam, between the inner and outer fabrics so that two edges of one face the front and two edges of the other face the back of the bag. Pin fabric edges together around the perimeter of the bag opening.

12. Beginning at a side seam, stitch a ½-inch (1.3 cm) seam around the tote, leaving a 5-inch (13 cm) opening. Pull both fabrics and straps through the gap, turning the tote bag right-side out, and press with an iron to remove any wrinkles. Topstitch around the tote bag's entire top edge to close the opening and finish the edges. This will also help reinforce the straps.

13. I decorated the bag with an anchor shape from a die-cut. If you don't have access to a die-cut machine, you can print a design from online and use it as a pattern.

Planter Pincushion

This fun and simple project was created for less than a dollar and makes a colorful statement on your sewing table. The whimsical pincushion was created with a thrift store planter purchased for twenty-five cents, a little fiberfill, and permanent fabric adhesive. Shopping thrift stores or church sales really helps keep costs low, and I get to feel good because I am giving something discarded a second chance with a new purpose.

MATERIALS

> › T-shirt scraps
> › Small ceramic planter
> › Fiberfill
> › Permanent fabric adhesive
> › Pencil
> › Scissors

INSTRUCTIONS

1. Wash and dry the planter before use. There was some questionable grime in the bottom of my planter, and I really had to scrub to remove it. Once the container was thoroughly clean, I allowed it to dry for an hour to make sure the ceramic had not absorbed any water and to ensure the glue would securely adhere.

2. Place the top of the planter on the T-shirt scrap and trace around the opening, leaving $1/2$ inch (1.3 cm) extra. Cut out the shape with a pair of scissors.
3. Fill the planter about two-thirds full with the fiberfill.
4. Run a line of glue around two-thirds of the inside edge of the planter. Place the T-shirt circle into the glue around the edge, leaving a small opening to add in more fiberfill.
5. Add more fiberfill until the top is slightly bulging, then add glue around the remainder of the opening and press the T-shirt material into the glue to securely close the opening.

Chevron Handbag

The summer I was in fifth grade, my midwestern family packed the Travelall and headed west for a joyful few weeks of family bonding along Route 66. That vacation took a wonderful turn just outside Albuquerque, New Mexico. We stopped at a roadside diner that looked like it had been abandoned; if it were not for the neon Open sign that fizzled in and out, we would have driven past. Not only was the food amazing and the pies on display picture-perfect, but there also was a back-room gift shop with handmade coats, hats, scarves, purses, and too many other items to list. The sister of the diner's owner was an artist who tooled leather and suede, painted fabric, and wove the most magnificent items that my eleven-year-old eyes had ever seen. I wanted to stay and watch her work her magic. Knowing I could not leave without something she created, I purchased a little tan leather coin pouch with flowers painted in the colors you see in my painted shoulder bag. The little coin pouch made it to college with me and was loved and used until it could no longer be repaired. The color combination has been one of my favorites to use in my art.

MATERIALS

> Denim scraps
> Hand-drawn pattern or purchased pattern of your choice
> Shannon Fabrics Cuddle Suede in Beige
> Fairfield Stiffen interfacing (to give body and structure)
> Iron and pressing cloth
> Scissors
> Rotary cutter, ruler, and mat (optional)
> Sewing machine
> Straight pins
> Denim needle
> Jean-A-Ma-Jig
> Heavy-duty thread
> Two 2-inch (5 cm) D-rings
> Stencil and stencil brush
> DecoArt Americana Acrylic Paint in Sea Breeze, Deep Midnight Blue, Coral Blush, and Sea Glass
> Optional: lining fabric; beads, jump rings, and headpins for the hanging trinket; jewelry pliers

INSTRUCTIONS

1. Draw your own pattern on brown craft paper or purchase a favorite handbag pattern. I made the bottom wider than the top and checked to make sure my laptop would fit in the bag along with a few other items.
2. Iron the Stiffen interfacing to the wrong side of the fabric. Stitch the two outside pieces together along three sides, right sides together, leaving the top open.

3. Reinforce the corners by stitching along the same line again. Repeat this step for the side pieces and lining.
4. Turn the bag right-side out and press. Pin a loop of the Cuddle suede on each side to hold the D-rings.
5. Place the stencil on the fabric and, with a stencil brush, coat the areas desired with the Deep Midnight Blue. Make sure to leave openings for the other colors. Repeat this step for each color. Allow the paint to dry.

8. To make the hanging trinket, place beads on the headpin. Once the headpin is full, use pliers to form a loop at the end. Place a jump ring on the end and place on the tote. Repeat to add as many pieces to the trinket as you would like.

TIPS

›› Trim the corners by snipping small Vs out of the seam allowance. This will give you a smooth curve when you turn the purse right-side out.

›› The iron is your friend; ironing is really important to get a crisp look.

6. Place the lining over the outside of the bag, with the right sides of the fabric together. Pin in place and stitch, making sure to leave a gap big enough to turn the fabric. Topstitch close to the edge to close the gap.

7. To make the strap, press the fabric in along the length on both sides, then fold in half along the length and topstitch along both sides. I wanted to leave my edges raw and fuzzy so I folded the Cuddle suede over 1 inch (3 cm) at each end of the strap, then pinned and stitched it in place about 5 inches (13 cm) from the top edge. Check that you haven't twisted the strap before you stitch.

Baby Bibs

This is quite possibly the easiest baby bib you will ever make—so easy you can make dozens in a day. Denim is a very durable material and only gets better with washing. The key to this project is the Sizzix die-cut and die-cut machine. You can literally crank out two at a time in a matter of minutes. If you don't have a Sizzix, you can trace around a bib on a piece of paper to make a pattern. You can get four or more bibs from a deconstructed pair of adult jeans (more if they are larger or longer). You can line the back of the bib with T-shirt material and make it reversible if you choose.

MATERIALS

› Two pieces of 9- by 12-inch (23 by 30 cm) denim or T-shirt fabric
› Fusible fleece
› Scissors
› Rotary cutter, ruler, and mat (optional)
› Sewing machine
› Heavy-duty thread
› Jean-A-Ma-Jig
› Iron and ironing surface
› Sizzix Big Shot Plus or Big Shot Pro die-cut machine (optional)
› Sizzix Baby Bib die (#660924) and Heart die #6 (#660789, optional)
› Embroidery floss
› Plastic snaps and snap setting tool

INSTRUCTIONS

1. Cut fabric to fit the size of the die-cut—approximately 9 by 12 inches (23 by 30 cm)—or cut each bib individually. Run the fabric through the die-cut machine following manufacturer's directions. Remove the cut fabric. If you are using the denim as a single-layer bib, sew a 1/4-inch (0.6 cm) seam around the edges to prevent excessive fraying. Add the decorative stitching in a contrasting thread color. To make a T-shirt version, place an additional layer of the T-shirt material behind the denim and sew with the stitch of your choice. You can go with a raw edge and sew in 1/4 inch (0.6 cm) or use a serger.

2. Use the snaps and snap setting tool following the manufacturer's directions to set the snap. Snaps come in a wide variety of colors. You can find them in the baby section at most craft stores or online.

Embellishments

1. To embellish with T-shirt accents: Place the fabric face up, then iron the fabric to the textured side of the fusible fleece following the manufacturer's directions. Run the layers through the die-cut machine and remove. Place the new shapes on the front of the bib and iron in place.

2. Decorative hand-stitching and machine-stitching can also be added. Play with the fancy stitches on your sewing machine. If you don't have extra stitches, you can add some stitch detail by hand or sew on some pretty ribbons. When using a button on baby clothing, make sure the button is sewn on extremely well.

Tote for Kids

Pint-size totes are very helpful when you are on the go. Children can be responsible for carrying their own items—one less thing for the adult to worry about. Making the drawstring backpack from clothes that no longer fit makes it a lot easier to part with if lost. Create a simple drawstring pouch from a patterned T-shirt for an adult day pack that will hold a water bottle, a cell phone, and a snack.

MATERIALS

> - T-shirt
> - Cotton cording
> - Scissors
> - Rotary cutter, ruler, and mat (optional but recommended)
> - Straight pins
> - Heavy-duty thread
> - Safety pin
> - Sewing machine

INSTRUCTIONS

1. Cut off both sleeves on the T-shirt, then cut horizontally across the top of the shirt, under the collar. Cut off about the bottom third of the shirt. Square up the layers with a ruler and rotary cutter for best accuracy. If you don't have these items, use a ruler and pencil.

2. Cut the seam off the bottom piece of fabric. Cut the smaller rectangle into four strips. The strips will form the loops of the backpack.

3. Pin the right sides (front) of the larger rectangle together so when you sew the bag it will be inside out.

4. Make two small loops on the bottom sides to hold the roping. These will be pinned inside the layers before sewing so that when you flip them, they will be on the outside.

5. Sew the sides together, but make sure to leave about 1½ to 2 inches (1.3 to 5 cm) at the top. Use a seam allowance of ⅝ inch (1.6 cm). You can change the size of the opening depending on the size of your cording. Remember to sew the seam allowance down all the way to the top even though the last 2 inches (5 cm) are not sewn together.

6. To attach the straps, fold the top down by about an inch (3 cm), pin and sew, leaving an opening at the top for the straps to go through. Repeat on both sides.

7. Using a safety pin attached to one of the straps, feed it through one side and then the other. Pull it until it is even and repeat with the other strap. To attach the straps to the bottom loops, pull through and knot.

Pretty Patterned Headband

With the leftover fabric from the Tote for Kids on page 20, you can also make a coordinating headband. This child-size pattern can be adjusted to fit by changing the length of the fold-over elastic that is used. This is a fast and easy sewing project that you can make in about a half hour. Once you get the hang of the pattern, you can make them in all kinds of fabric combinations and give them as gifts. They are also great items to sell at craft shows, and have been one of my best sellers since 2013. The style is classic, and you can stay on trend with your color combinations and fabric choices.

Note: I like to use fusible fleece on the inside to give them more bulk. This is completely optional. If you choose to use fusible fleece, iron it to the wrong side of one of the fabric pieces and follow the rest of the directions.

MATERIALS

> › T-shirt scrap
> › Fold-over elastic
> › Scissors
> › Rotary cutter, ruler, and mat (optional)
> › Straight pins
> › Heavy-duty thread
> › Fusible fleece and iron (optional)

INSTRUCTIONS

1. Fold fabric and place the wide end of the template on the fold. Cut two pieces of the fabric.
2. Cut a 7- to 9-inch (18 to 23 cm) piece of fold-over elastic.
3. Place the right sides of the fabric together. Fold down $1/4$ inch (0.6 cm) on both pieces of fabric on one end of the headband and iron.
4. Slide in the fold-over elastic between the fabric pieces.
5. Pin the pieces together.
6. Starting at the end of the headband without the fold-over elastic, sew from the open end all the way around until you reach the opening again.
7. Pull the headband right-side out by pulling the inner fabric through the open end of the headband.
8. Iron the headband flat. Iron in $1/4$ inch (0.6 cm) on the open end of the headband.
9. Slip the fold-over elastic in the opening (about $1/2$ inch/1.3 cm). Sew the opening closed.
10. Topstitch all the way around the headband for a clean, finished look.

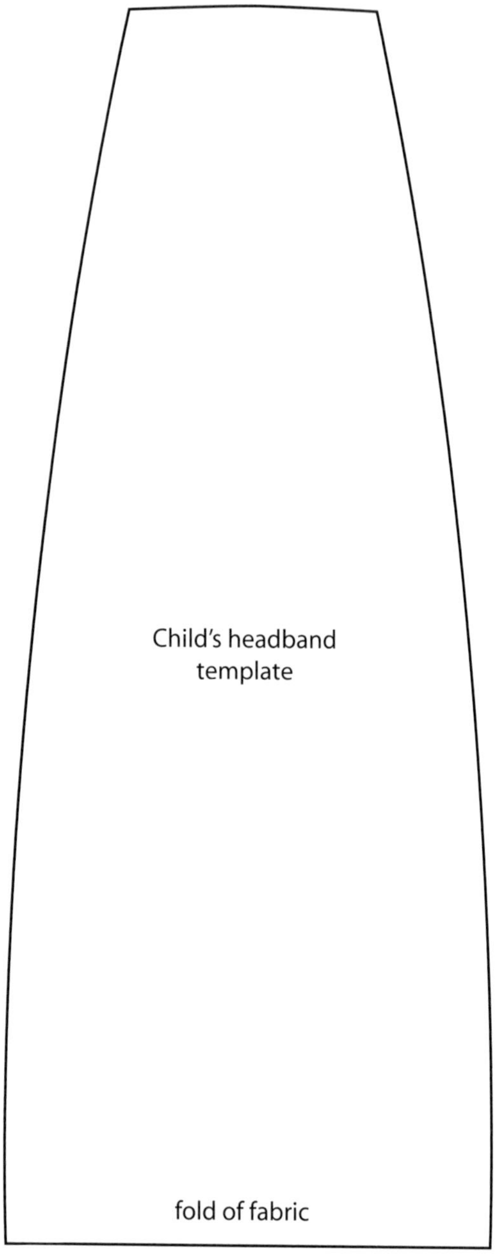

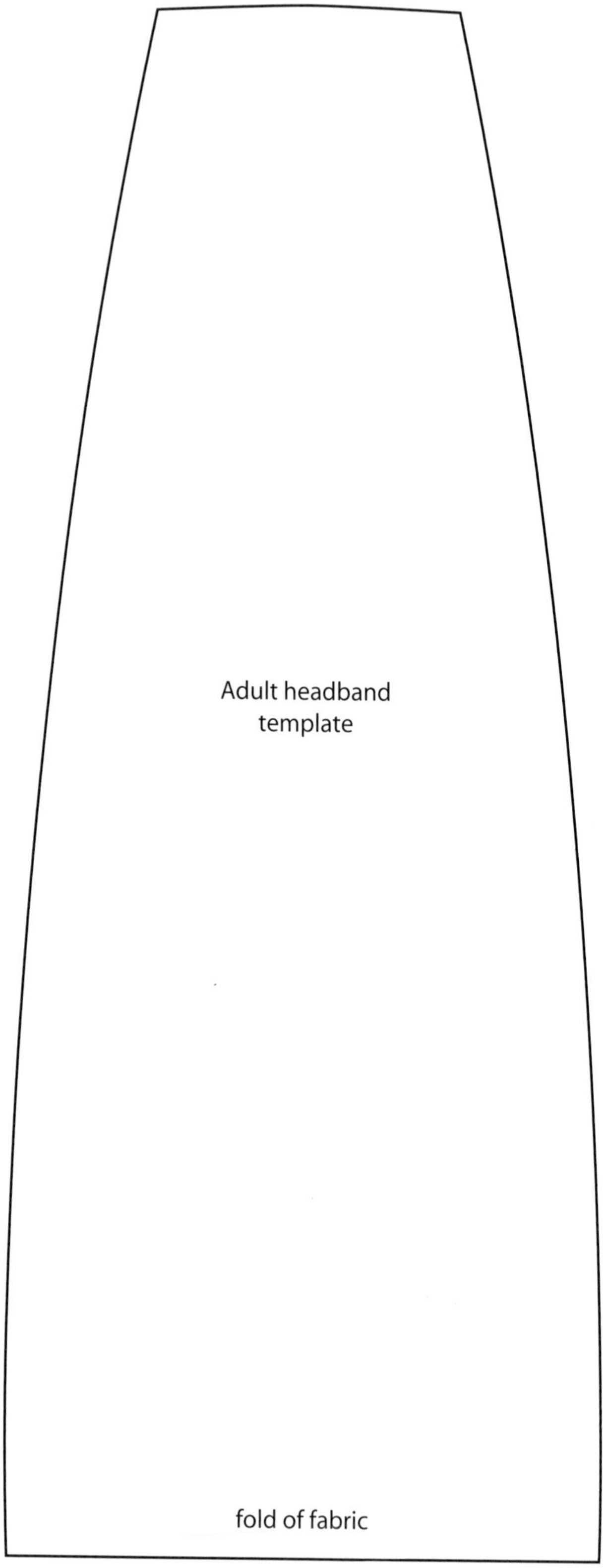

Adult headband
template

Child's headband
template

fold of fabric

fold of fabric

Stitch and
Slash Pillow

The free-flow style of "stitch and slash" is very forgiving. This style of fabric manipulation works great with T-shirts because of their weave. When you make your first slash in the fabric, it develops a delightful roll that makes each piece unique. I like to draw where my slashes are going to be so they are evenly spaced. This same method can be used with layers of cotton to create a chenille look. Different fabrics give different results. I encourage you to have fun and play around with this technique.

MATERIALS

> T-shirt scraps in six to eight colors
> Fusible fleece
> Heavy-duty thread
> Pencil
> Thread to match fabric
> Straight pins
> Scissors
> Rotary cutter, ruler, and mat (optional)
> Iron and ironing surface
> Fiberfill

INSTRUCTIONS

1. Layer two pieces of T-shirt fabric together, right sides up. I used rectangles approximately 6 by 10 inches (15 by 25 cm). Sew the layers together and stitch over your lines twice.

2. On the right side, draw lines where you want to cut. These will be hidden when the fabric rolls. Leave 1 or 2 inches (3 or 5 cm) between each drawn line.

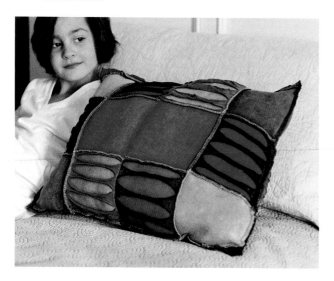

3. Pinch the top layer and pull it away from the bottom layer. Snip a small hole in the top layer only and cut along the drawn lines.

4. Repeat this technique with different color combinations until you have enough pieces for the size pillow you want. (I used this method for both sides of this pillow.)

5. Sew the rectangles together with wrong sides facing each other. This creates a raw edge. Feel free to create a few extra stitch lines, as this adds to the rustic nature of the pillow.

6. After the top is complete, cover it with a layer of batting (I like to use fusible fleece).

7. Cut a piece of fabric for the back of the pillow the same size as the front. Place front and back pieces wrong sides together. Sew along the outer edges using a ½-inch (1.3 cm) seam allowance. Leave a small opening on one side large enough to add the fiberfill.

8. Wash separately in a washing machine and then dry. Turn inside out and iron the edges open. Turn the pillow right-side out and carefully use the tip of a chopstick to push the corners of the pillow out.

9. To avoid lumps when stuffing your pillow, use this method: Start with a generous handful of filling. Gently pull the filling loose. The idea is to remove any clumps, while fluffing the fill at the same time. Repeat the process two to three times before inserting the fill into your project. Start stuffing the worked fill into one of the corners farthest from the seam opening. It is best to work your way out. Gently but firmly push the fill into the corner. Pay attention to the outside as you go—you can see any lumps or indents forming. Add filling to the area to smooth out the surface, or remove some filling and "work it" more to remove a stubborn clump. Once the corners are filled, insert small amounts of additional fill.

10. To hand-sew the opening closed, thread the needle with coordinating thread. Keeping your stitches as small as possible, slip-stitch the opening closed. The tiny stitches help to ensure no stuffing will poke out of the hand-sewn seam.

Denim Scrap Pillow

To make the pattern on this pillow, you will need to cut a variety of denim fabric into 3- by 6-inch (8 by 15 cm) rectangles. If you use a rotary cutter it will go much faster, your lines will be straighter, and the corners will line up—trust me on this one; there are thirty rectangles for one pillow (you can change the dimensions to fit your needs). Make sure your seams are tight to help with alignment.

MATERIALS

› Denim scraps in various shades
› One 30- by 18-inch (76 by 46 cm) piece of denim
› Scissors
› Rotary cutter, ruler, and mat (optional but recommended)
› Sewing machine and coordinating thread
› Straight pins
› Jean-A-Ma-Jig
› Iron and ironing surface
› Fiberfill
› Needle and thread

INSTRUCTIONS

1. Iron material before cutting. This will help to keep corners clean and everything lined up.
2. Cut thirty rectangles measuring 3 by 6 inches (8 by 15 cm) from several shades of denim fabric.
3. You can make a pattern with your different colored scraps or make three stacks of ten and use them randomly. (I chose random.)
4. Place two pieces of fabric right sides together and sew along the 6-inch side using a $1/2$-inch (1.3 cm) seam allowance. Repeat until you have sewn all ten pieces in the stack into a long strip. Repeat for each stack of rectangles.
5. Place the first strip right-side down and iron all the seams open. Repeat for the other two strips.
6. Right sides together, position two fabric strips so that the seams align. Pin in place and sew the strips together lengthwise. Repeat for the remaining strip. Press open all seams.
7. Cut a piece of fabric for the back of the pillow the same size as the front. Place front and back pieces right sides together. Sew along the outer edge using a $1/2$-inch (1.3 cm) seam allowance. Leave a small opening on one side large enough to add the fiberfill.

8. Once the pieces are sewn together, you need to clip the edges. Make clips in the fabric about $1/4$ inch (0.6 cm) apart along all seams. *Do not* cut too close to the seam lines.
9. Wash separately in a washing machine and then dry. Turn inside out and iron the edges open. Turn the pillow right-side out and carefully use the tip of a chopstick to push the corners of the pillow out.
10. To avoid lumps when stuffing your pillow, use this method: Start with a generous handful of filling. Gently pull the filling loose. The idea is to remove any clumps, while fluffing the fill at the same time. Repeat the process two to three times before inserting the fill into your project. Start stuffing the worked fill into one of the corners farthest from the seam opening. It is best to work your way out. Gently but firmly push the fill into the corner. Pay attention to the outside as you go—you can see any lumps or indents forming. Add filling to the immediate area to smooth out the surface, or remove some filling and "work it" more to remove a stubborn clump. Once the corners are filled, insert small amounts of additional fill.
11. To hand-sew the opening closed, thread the needle with coordinating thread. Keeping your stitches as small as possible, slip-stitch the opening closed. The tiny stitches help to ensure no stuffing will poke out of the hand-sewn seam.

Cathedral Window Table Runner

This decorative table runner made from denim and T-shirts is inspired by an old quilt block. The circle/square design is also called circular patchwork, folded cottage windows, mock cathedral windows, and faux cathedral windows. The piece is time consuming to prepare but relatively easy to assemble. You can determine the size of your pattern by the size of the circle you use to trace around for the pieces. This runner was made using large-mouth mason jar rings. If you want a larger look, you can use a small plate; for a smaller design try a standard-size mason jar ring or a soup can. But remember, the smaller the size the more cutting and sewing. Decide on the length and width you want. I'm not one for following rules, so I usually end up winging it.

TIP: Table runners come in standard widths from 10 to 15 inches (25 to 38 cm) wide and standard lengths from 36 to 108 inches (0.9 to 2.7 m) long. The width of your table runner should be approximately one-third the width of your table. For a formal table setting, the length should allow for 6 inches (15 cm) to hang over each end. For a smaller table runner as shown, size it to fit as desired.

MATERIALS

> Denim scraps
> T-shirt scraps
> Scissors
> Rotary cutter, ruler, and mat (optional but recommended)
> Jean-A-Ma-Jig
> Thread
> Pins
> Fusible fleece (optional)
> Iron and ironing surface
> Circle template
> Square template
> Glue stick

INSTRUCTIONS

1. To make the cathedral windows runner, first decide on the size circle you want. Then mark off a square in the center.
2. Measure the size of the square and then make a template out of a cereal box to use for the square.
3. Cut circles out of the denim. I usually make a few extra just in case I mess up.
4. To make the squares for inside the window, I typically iron fusible fleece on the wrong side of a large piece of T-shirt material. This makes the T-shirt material more stable and easier to work with. You can draw on the fabric and then cut out the shapes. (I like to use my ruler and rotary cutter to save time.)
5. Once you have all the circles cut out, trace your square *on every circle*. This will be your guide when sewing the circles together and also when placing the T-shirt squares. Do not skip this step!
6. Begin by stitching two denim circles together on the marked lines. The rounded edges of the circles become flaps. Work in rows to complete the base.
7. Insert a square of T-shirt fabric in each "window" and secure with a glue stick. Fold the flaps over the scraps and stitch down the raw edges of the flaps, stitching through all the layers. Repeat until you complete the piece.

Shirred and Blocked Floor Pillow

Shirring is an old technique that has been made easier using iron-on shirring tape, which is a really cool product that's fairly undiscovered. It's super easy to use and lets you make soft pleats on fabric panels with no sewing required. While I love sewing, sometimes it is nice to skip a time-consuming step. The shirring adds an extra detail to the floor pillow and allows it a bit of extra give. When shirring, cut panels one and a half to two times the desired finished length—you can always trim off the excess, and it is very difficult to add more once you start. To make the pillow the same size as mine, use the measurements below, but feel free to change it up to fit your needs. I love to use a variety of quilting and sewing rulers; in fact, I often call them templates because that is how I use them. I place them on my cutting mat and use a rotary cutter to cut along each side to get a perfect square.

MATERIALS

- › Thirty-two 10½-inch (26.5 cm) denim squares in a variety of colors
- › Four strips of T-shirt material approximately 64 inches (163 cm) long and 6 inches (15 cm) wide each
- › Jean-A-Ma-Jig
- › Iron-on shirring tape
- › Dritz Ezy-Hem gauge
- › Easy Grasp pins
- › Scissors
- › Rotary cutter, ruler, and mat (optional but recommended)
- › Thread
- › Fusible fleece (optional)
- › Iron and ironing surface
- › Fiberfill

INSTRUCTIONS

1. Once you have the needed fabric pieces cut, place two squares right sides together and sew using a ½-inch (1.3 cm) seam allowance. Repeat until you have four pieces to form a strip.
2. Sew the four strips together in the same manner. Repeat for the other side of the pillow.
3. Make the shirred strips using the T-shirts strips and iron-on shirring tape, following the manufacturer's directions. If you are using fusible fleece, adhere it to the wrong side of the shirred strips and trim off excess fleece.

4. Attach the shirred strips to the first blocked panel by placing the right sides together and sewing along the outer edge using a ½-inch (1.3 cm) seam allowance. Sew a strip on all four sides.
5. Attach the top panel using the same method, but only sewing on three of the four sides. On the fourth side, leave a seam along the outer edge using a ½-inch (1.3 cm) seam allowance. Leave a small opening on one side large enough to add the fiberfill.
6. Turn the pillow right-side out and carefully use the tip of a chopstick to push the corners of the pillow out.
7. To avoid lumps when stuffing your pillow, use this method: Start with a generous handful of filling. Gently pull the filling loose. The idea is to remove any clumps, while fluffing the fill at the same time. Repeat the process two to three times before inserting the fill into your project. Start stuffing the worked fill into one of the corners farthest

from the seam opening. It is best to work your way out. Gently but firmly push the fill into the corner. Pay attention to the outside as you go—you can see any lumps or indents forming. Add filling to the immediate area to smooth out the surface, or remove some filling and "work it" more to remove a stubborn clump. Once the corners are filled, insert small amounts of additional fill.

8. To hand-sew the opening closed, thread the needle with coordinating thread. Keeping your stitches as small as possible, slip-stitch the opening closed. The tiny stitches help to ensure no stuffing will poke out of the hand-sewn seam.

Tech Pillow

Holding a phone or tablet while watching videos or playing games can strain your arms or neck. To help hold your device upright, use a tech pillow. A tech pillow does not have to cost an arm and a leg and can be made with a leftover T-shirt or jeans. This pillow has a special feature—it is weighted with Poly-Pellets. The extra weight on the bottom gives it stability, and when kids are using them they need all the extra support they can get. I make a paper funnel to get the pellets into the opening.

MATERIALS

> One 5- by 14- inch (13 by 36 cm) T-shirt scrap
> Scissors
> Rotary cutter, ruler, and mat (optional)
> Thread
> Pins
> Fusible fleece and iron (optional)
> Fiberfill
> Fairfield Poly-Pellets

The T-shirt used for this project, prior to cutting.

INSTRUCTIONS

1. Cut the fabric to a 5- by 14-inch (13 by 36 cm) rectangle. Fold the fabric in half with wrong sides out. If you are using fusible fleece, adhere to the fabric before cutting.
2. Pin and sew the two sides closed. Turn the fabric right-side out.
3. Using the paper funnel, add $1/4$ cup Poly-Pellets to fill the bottom inch of the pouch.
4. Form a roll across the bottom of the pouch where the Poly-Pellets are by pinning across the pouch and sewing the two sides together. This will create the base for the tech pillow.
5. Add fiberfill to fill the rest of the bag. If you want to give it additional weight, you can add more pellets.
6. Bring the sewn edges of the bag together. Turn the sides in approximately $1/2$ inch (1.3 cm).
7. Pin the sides together to close the bag. Sew the sides together to seal the bag.

Crochet
Accent Rug

Denim makes great yarn to use in crochet projects. It is durable, a classic color, and looks better with each wash. The rug shown took approximately four pairs of jeans to make. The denim yarn was wrapped in a ball in random order so the rug would have a variegated color. You can use contrasting colors or all one color to fit your needs.

MATERIALS

> Denim from four to five pairs of jeans
> Scissors
> Rotary cutter, ruler, and mat (optional but recommended)
> Crochet hook, US size N, O, P, or Q (10–16 mm)

INSTRUCTIONS

Make the Denim Yarn

1. Cut straight across the jean leg, just below the back pocket. Do the same for both sides. The top part of the jeans where the waist/pockets/zipper is will not be used for this project (save for other projects).
2. Cut the hem off the bottom of the pant leg, as it is too bulky for this use (save for the Dazzling Dog Collar project on page 68).
3. To maximize the yarn that you can get out of your jean legs use the following method with either scissors or a rotary cutter. I use my rotary cutter because it is faster and I am comfortable with it. (I cannot stress enough to make sure you take safety precautions when working with a rotary cutter.)
4. Cut the strips the length of the jean leg, leaving approximately two fingers width from the inside leg seam, but do not cut through the inside leg seam. You can cut the strips to whatever width you want, in this case about 1 inch (3 cm) wide.
5. The strips can be cut by eye, as it doesn't have to be very accurate. Keep repeating this cut along the pant leg. The result will be lots of loops that resemble fringe.

6. Start on the first loop. Cut one end of the loop so that it turns the loop into a length of denim yarn. Continue in this way, making a series of diagonal cuts that will join the strips together, turning the fringes into continuous yarn.

7. Once the strips are cut, you will need to attach them together. Cut a 1-inch (3 cm) slit (lengthwise) in the end of each strip. Lay the end of one strip over the top of the end of another strip, with the holes aligned. Then take the other end of the strip that is lying on top and from the bottom pull that strip through the slits. Carefully pull it tight to make a strong and not very noticeable joint.

8. Repeat until all the pieces are joined. Roll the giant strip into a ball. (I made six to seven balls using four to five pairs of pants.) You can get a lot attached together before you start crocheting (and wind the strip in a ball), or you can join the strips together as you need them.

Crochet the Rug

Chain 8, join to form a ring.

Round 1: Chain 5, double crochet in same chain. Skip next chain, chain 2. [(Double crochet, chain 2, double crochet) in next chain, skip next chain, chain 2] around. Join with slip stitch in third chain of beginning chain-5.

Round 2: Chain 5, do not turn. Double crochet in same stitch, chain 2. [(Double crochet, chain 2, double crochet) in next double crochet, chain 2] around. Join with slip stitch in third chain of beginning chain-5.

Round 3: Chain 3 (double crochet, chain 2, double crochet) in next chain-2 space. [Double crochet in next 2 double crochet (double crochet, chain 2, double crochet) in next chain-2 space] around to last double crochet. Double crochet in last double crochet. Join with slip stitch in top of beginning chain-3.

Round 4 and all following rows until you reach desired size: Chain 3, double crochet in each double crochet (double crochet, chain 2, double crochet) in each chain-2 space around. Join with slip stitch in top of beginning chain 3.

Diamond Pillow

This pillow uses a similar blocking method as the Shirred and Blocked Floor Pillow on page 31. The only difference in the blocking method is that the blocks are turned at an angle and the excess is trimmed off. Working with blocks can be fun if you like working with graphic patterns. My style is loose and relaxed, and if something is not perfect I am okay with it. I encourage you to be open to results that are not what you were expecting.

MATERIALS

> Denim scraps, 8 by 8 inches (20 by 20 cm)
> Scissors
> Rotary cutter, ruler, and mat (optional but recommended)
> Thread
> Pins
> Iron and ironing surface
> Jean-A-Ma-Jig
> Fiberfill

INSTRUCTIONS

1. Once you have the needed fabric pieces cut, place two squares right side together and sew using a 1/2-inch (1.3 cm) seam allowance. Repeat until you have four pieces to form a strip.

2. Sew the four strips together in the same manner. Repeat for the other side of the pillow. Turn the fabric so that diamonds are formed and not squares. Square up the fabric panel by trimming off the excess.

3. Cut a piece of fabric for the back of the pillow the same size as the front. Place right sides together. Sew along the outer edges using a 1/2-inch (1.3 cm) seam allowance. Leave a small opening on one side large enough to add the fiberfill.

4. Once the pieces are sewn together, you need to clip the edges. Make clips in the fabric about 1/4 inch (0.6 cm) apart along all seams. *Do not* cut too close to the seam lines.

5. Wash separately in a washing machine and then dry. Turn inside out and iron the edges open. Turn the pillow right-side out and carefully use the tip of a chopstick to push the corners of the pillow out.

6. To avoid lumps when stuffing your pillow, use this method: Start with a generous handful of filling. Gently pull the filling loose. The idea is to remove any clumps, while fluffing the fill at the same time. Repeat the process two to three times before inserting the fill into your project. Start stuffing the worked fill into one of the corners farthest from the seam opening. It is best to work your way out. Gently but firmly push the fill into the corner. Pay attention to the outside as you go—you can see any lumps or indents forming. Add filling to the immediate area to smooth out the surface, or remove some filling and "work it" more to remove a stubborn clump. Once the corners are filled, insert small amounts of additional fill.

7. To hand-sew the opening closed, thread the needle with coordinating thread. Keeping your stitches as small as possible, slip-stitch the opening closed. The tiny stitches help to ensure no stuffing will poke out of the hand-sewn seam.

Director's Chair

irect your life in style from this quick-to-make and simple-to-assemble director's chair.

I found a pair of chairs that were in good shape at the thrift store for five dollars. I sanded and painted them with an outdoor spray paint in white (only one of the chairs is shown in the photos). We plan to use these chairs as part of our camping gear and co-ordinate with the Hammock Cover featured on page 49.

MATERIALS

> Denim fabric
> Scissors
> Rotary cutter, ruler, and mat (optional)
> Heavy-duty thread
> Pins
> Jean-A-Ma-Jig
> Iron and ironing surface
> Tape measure

INSTRUCTIONS

1. Measure the opening of your director's chair or the fabric that was on it for the top and the bottom to get an accurate measurement for your fabric. Add 4 inches (10 cm) additional material for each side that wraps around the post on the top. You can trim off any excess. For the top and bottom panel add an extra 2 inches (5 cm), which will give you enough for a ½-inch (1.3 cm) seam allowance and room to trim off the excess if desired. It is easier to cut off excess than to try and add more at the end.

2. Since the panel is being made with fabric scraps, use any combination of leftover pieces to create the panel dimensions. Use a ½-inch (1.3 cm) seam allowance for the rag quilt style. This will give you a nice edge all the way around. Sew fabric pieces together with heavy-duty thread and sew around every seam an extra time or two. (If I am sitting in a chair, I want to know it is going to hold me.) Using a ½-inch (1.3 cm) seam allowance, sew the blocks in each row together. Attach rows to each other, placing rows wrong sides together and matching seam intersections. When the fabric panel is complete, sew a seam around the entire piece.

3. Wash the pieces to fray the edges. Attach to the chair frame and then sit back and enjoy.

Embroidered Body Pillow

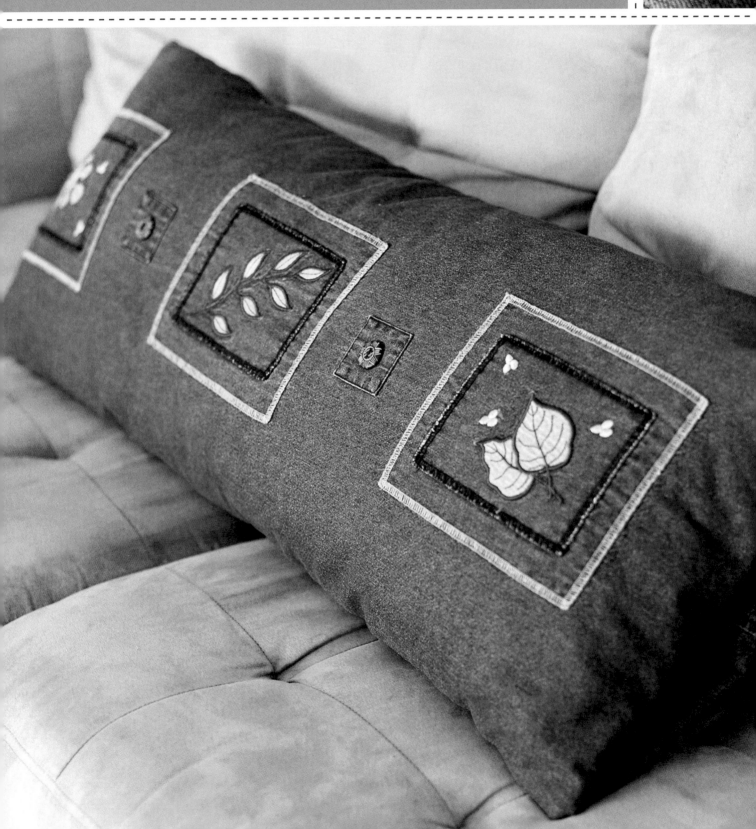

This pretty embroidered pillow practically made itself. I came across a large-size denim dress from the 1980s—the kind that sweet elementary schoolteachers wore because they were comfortable and durable and all the rage at the time. With the volume of fabric that came with the dress and the embroidered accents down the front, I knew it would make a great bench pillow or even a body pillow. You can use this design as inspiration and add your own details to the three blocks.

MATERIALS

> One 16- by 38-inch (41 by 97 cm) pillow form
> One 17- by 39-inch (43 by 99 cm) fabric panel
> One 17- by 39-inch (43 by 99 cm) backing fabric panel
> 1¼ yards (1.14 meters) fusible interfacing
> Thread to match fabric
> Scissors
> Rotary cutter, ruler, and mat (optional)
> Jean-A-Ma-Jig

INSTRUCTIONS

1. Cut four rectangles, 17 by 39 inches (43 by 99 cm), two from the fabric and two from the interfacing. For best results align the embroidered pieces so they will be centered on the fabric.
2. Following the manufacturer's directions, fuse interfacing to the back of the pillow front and to the wrong side of the backing fabric.
3. Place right sides together. Stitch around the outside edge of the pillow using a ½-inch (1.3 cm) seam. Repeat stitching ¼ inch (0.6 cm) away from the first row of stitching for additional strength. Leave enough room on one end to fit the pillow form into the pillow. Clip the excess fabric from the pillow corners. Turn right-side out and press. Insert the pillow form.
4. To hand-sew the opening closed, thread a needle with coordinating thread. Keeping your stitches as small as possible, slip-stitch the opening closed.

Laundry Bag

For this very durable laundry bag, I used long, wide strips of denim and my son's initials in 3-inch iron-on varsity block letters. Ideally this bag will last through four years of summer camp and four years of college. If it does last eight years, the nice thing is that since it is denim, it will never go out of style. You can adjust the size of the bag to fit your needs (I needed it to hold two weeks' worth of clothes). The base circle is 12 inches (30 cm) in diameter. The fabric tube is 37 by 33 inches (94 by 84 cm), and the finished size of the tube is 36 by 32 inches (91 by 81 cm) (the measurements allow for seam allowances).

MATERIALS

> Denim fabric
> Heavy-duty thread to match fabric
> Straight pins
> Scissors
> Rotary cutter, ruler, and mat (optional)
> Jean-A-Ma-Jig
> Iron and ironing surface
> Roping
> Optional: iron-on 3-inch varsity block letters

INSTRUCTIONS

1. Cut a circle 13 inches (33 cm) around and set aside (the finished piece will be 12 inches/30 cm).
2. Cut and sew together strips of denim to form a piece of fabric that is 37 by 33 inches (94 by 84 cm). (My fabric has three rows of fabric pieces set horizontally and one row of fabric pieces set vertically.)
3. Pin and sew the right sides together, making sure to leave about 1½ to 2 inches (3.8 to 5 cm) at the top. Use a ½-inch (1.3 cm) seam allowance. You can change the size of the opening depending on the size of your roping. Remember to sew the seam allowance down all the way to the top even though the last 2 inches (5 cm) are not sewn together.
4. Fold the top down by about 1½ inches (3.8 cm), pin, and sew, leaving an opening at the top for the roping to go through.
5. Using a safety pin attached to one end of the roping, feed it through one side and out the other. Pull it until it is even and tie a knot on each end. Add glue to the knot if desired.
6. Turn the tube inside out. Pin the 13-inch (33 cm) circle into place and sew around the base slowly, which will alleviate puckers. Make sure you use a small stitch and heavy-duty thread, since this is the bottom of the bag.
7. Iron on the letters in the location of your choice.

Pocketed Floor Pouf

M y rowdy kids love this piece and it gets used daily. It works as a footstool, a bean bag for the youngest, and a back rest for both. The addition of pockets makes it extra functional. This is another piece that you can make any size you want (mine is approximately 18 inches [46 cm] tall and 24 inches [61 cm] wide).

MATERIALS

› Denim fabric
› Thread to match fabric
› Straight pins
› Scissors
› Rotary cutter, ruler, and mat (optional)
› Jean-A-Ma-Jig
› Bean bag filler (I used 1.5 bags)

INSTRUCTIONS

1. Cut fabric into strips 7 by 20 inches (18 by 51 cm) for the sides and 7 by 25 inches (18 by 64 cm) for the top and bottom. You will need 16 pieces for the sides and 8 pieces each for the top and bottom. Sew the pieces wrong sides together so you will have fringed edges. Use a $1/2$-inch (1.3 cm) seam allowance.
2. Sew the sides together to form a rectangle and then sew the top and the bottom pieces on. Leave an opening for the bean bag filler.
3. Pour in the filler following the manufacturer's instructions. This can be messy, so take your time on this step.
4. To hand-sew the opening closed, thread the needle with coordinating thread. Keeping your stitches as small as possible, slip-stitch the opening closed.

Hammock Cover

Taking a hammock camping is a necessity with my family. We are all readers, and one of our favorite things to do is take a rest break in the shade and read snuggled up in the hammock. This hammock cover keeps the hammock clean and is easy to remove for laundering. The cover comes off easily for storage thanks to the straps with buckles that are sewn to the edges. The buckles came from worn-out backpacks. If you cannot find any buckles and straps you can spare, both are sold in the notions aisle. When sewing the seams, feel free to go around them as many times as you want (at least two extra times to be sure the seams hold).

MATERIALS

> Denim fabric
> Heavy-duty thread to match fabric
> Straight pins
> Scissors
> Rotary cutter, ruler, and mat (optional but recommended)
> Jean-A-Ma-Jig
> 2 yards (1.8 m) black webbing, 1 inch (2.5 cm) wide
> Six 1-inch (2.5 cm) black parachute buckles

INSTRUCTIONS

1. For this project, the larger you make your squares, the quicker the cutting and sewing goes. I wish I would have made my squares bigger. Lesson learned! Make as many large pieces as you need for the size of your hammock.

2. After you have cut out the squares for the hammock, design your pattern and stack the pieces in rows according to pattern placement. If you are tight on space, hang a sheet on a wall and pin the pieces to the sheet to arrange. My dining room table doubles as my workspace when piecing together.

3. Gather the first two blocks in the first row. Place the blocks wrong sides together, noting which edges should be connected. Sew along the aligned edges with a 1/2-inch (1.3 cm) seam allowance.

4. Add the next block, again placing wrong sides together. Finish sewing the blocks in each row together. Attach rows to each other, placing rows wrong sides together and matching seam intersections.

5. When the cover is complete, sew a line of stitching around the entire piece, 1/2 inch (1.3 cm) from each side. If you stop 1/2 inch (1.3 cm) from the ends, backstitch at each angle of the corner.

6. Once the pieces are sewn together, you need to clip the edges to create the fringed look. Make perpendicular cuts about 1/4 inch (0.6 cm) apart along all seams. *Do not* cut too close to the seam lines. (I did this on a few and had to go in and repair them after washing. Another lesson learned.)

7. Toss in the washing machine on the heaviest cycle.

8. Cut the webbing into 12 6-inch (15.25 cm) pieces. (I used three straps on each end, as this was a good number to feel secure without sagging or extra movement.) Thread one piece of webbing through one side of a buckle and stitch down; repeat for the other side of the buckle with another webbing piece. Attach the straps to the hammock by sewing them on the edges.

Tank Top Tote

This tank top bag makes a super-stylish produce bag to carry to the farmer's market or grocery store. The fancy beadwork makes it a statement piece, too. The tank had stretched out and no longer fit my mother like she wanted, and she happily donated it to my stash of grocery bags until she saw how great it looked and reclaimed it for herself! This bag is so simple to make that you will be scouring your drawers for tank tops you no longer wear.

MATERIALS

> Tank top
> Thread
> Scissors
> Pins (optional)

INSTRUCTIONS

1. Are you ready for the instructions? Turn the tank top inside out and sew along the bottom in a straight line. Go over the seam a couple of times for added strength.
2. Turn the shirt right-side out and voila! You have a fancy produce bag.

Wine Bottle Cozy with T-shirt Flower

Straight leg or skinny leg jeans work best for this project. The T-shirt flower is a fun embellishment. I used an old bleached-out shirt and cut it into petal shapes, then used a stiffening liquid to create the flower. The liquid was fun and easy to use, and I have a bunch of ideas swirling in my head for different ways to use it.

MATERIALS

> T-shirt
> Scissors
> Rotary cutter, ruler, and mat (optional)
> Stiffen Stuff by Beacon Adhesives
> Dowel rod
> Wood button
> Jute cording
> Fabri-Tac fabric adhesive
> Jean-A-Ma-Jig

INSTRUCTIONS

Wine Cozy

1. Choose jeans with a leg opening about 6 inches (15 cm) wide. If you don't have any skinny jeans on hand, cut the leg and re-seam it smaller.
2. The average wine bottle is 13 inches (33 cm) tall, so cut the pant leg at 15 to 17 inches (38 to 43 cm). This will give you a 1-inch (3 cm) seam allowance and a bit extra at the top.
3. Use the bottom of the jeans as the top of the cozy, so you only need to sew one very short seam. Turn the leg wrong side out, sew the seam, trim off any excess, and turn the bag right-side out.
4. Insert the wine bottle. Tie the jute around the neck of the bottle.

T-shirt Flower

1. To make the flower, cut flower petals out of the T-shirt material in various sizes. The petals were cut out in a freeform style: ten each of small, medium, and large.
2. Use the fabric stiffener on the petals according to package directions. I allowed my petals to dry over a dowel rod to create a little curve.
3. Use hot glue or fabric glue to adhere the petals to the back of the wood button.

4. Glue the flower to the side of the jute knot.

Tablet Case

Transport and protect your electronic tablet with simplicity and style using this easy-sew case. By using a lightweight fusible batting to create this lightly padded case, it is easier than ever to hold the layers in place while sewing, and the use of the lightweight batting also helps to ensure protection from everyday bumps and scratches. The ability to customize this envelope-style case to genuinely express your own personal style lies in the choice of fabrics, trims, and notions selected. Due to the design utilizing multiple patterns of fabric, the options are truly endless. The simple design includes the addition and customization (size, shape, and number) of pockets, which allows this fabulous tablet case to meet all your function needs, too. This case can be created in just one afternoon, making it the perfect project to create for yourself or to give as a lovely handmade gift.

MATERIALS

> Fabric
> Fusible batting
> Thread to match fabric
> Velcro® Brand 1-inch square white sew-on fastener (optional)
> Scissors
> Ruler or tape measure
> Iron and ironing surface
> Sewing machine
> Straight pins and sewing needle

TIP: To adjust the measurements for any tablet or electronic device, take the measurements of the device and add 1½ to 2 inches (3.8 to 5 cm). If the piece is thick, add 2 inches. If it is thin, add 1½.

INSTRUCTIONS

1. For the layer with the fold-over flap (the longest piece), cut two pieces of fabric and one piece of the fusible batting to measure 9 by 15 inches (23 by 38 cm).

2. For the smaller layer, cut two pieces of fabric and one piece of fusible batting that measure 9 by 11 inches (23 by 28 cm).

3. Sew one side of the Velcro® square to the 9- by 11-inch outer piece. Then match it up with the inner piece that is 9 by 15 inches. You are sewing both of these on the right side of the fabric. They need to line up when the flap is folded down.

4. With the Velcro® square in place, iron the fusible fleece to the wrong side of the long and short lining pieces. Lift and press the iron instead of moving it back and forth, which will stretch the fabric.

5. With right sides together, pin the layers in place. Sew the two outer pieces together and the two inner pieces together. Leave one edge open on each piece so you can turn it right-side out. Trim off any excess fabric.

6. Turn both pieces right-side out and press flat.

7. Places the pieces together with the outside fabric on the inside. Start with the open edges and pin the two pieces together. Sew around three of the four edges to form the pouch. Trim off any excess from the bottom and press flat. Turn the pieces right-side out and press again.

T-shirt Yarn
Place Mat

trips from T-shirts that most would think unusable are perfect for this project. You can use any lap loom or small loom; there are many available in big box stores and online. If you have a small loom, weave and stitch several pieces together to make a larger piece. Make your own T-shirt yarn by cutting ³/₄- to 1-inch (1.9 to 3 cm) strips. For this project I used all the sleeves and top portions of shirts that I had set aside from pillow projects. If you want larger strips of T-shirt yarn, use the method described in the instructions. Apply the same technique to remnants.

MATERIALS

> 16- by 12-inch (41 by 30 cm) lap loom and supplies
> A variety of yarn made from T-shirt scraps
> Cotton yarn
> Scissors
> Rotary cutter, ruler, and mat (optional but recommended)

INSTRUCTIONS

T-shirt Yarn

1. Lay a T-shirt out on a work surface. Cut straight across under the sleeves, removing the neckline and sleeves from the shirt. Then cut the hem off the bottom of the shirt.
2. Fold one side of the T-shirt toward the other, leaving a 1-inch (3 cm) space at the top. Cut slits spaced ³/₄- to 1-inch (1.9 to 3 cm) apart from the side you just folded up to the space at the top, but do not cut all the way through the space at the top (this is what will hold your yarn together in one piece).
3. Unfold the shirt and cut the strips diagonally from one strip to the next. Starting on the first loop, cut one end of the loop so that it turns the loop into a strip of yarn. Repeat this step to form a continuous strip of yarn.
4. Pull the single strip of T-shirt yarn you cut through your hands—this causes the edges to curl and creates the tube shape. Keep pulling until it is all tube-shaped. Roll the T-shirt yarn into a ball. Repeat this process for as many colors as you want in your place mat.

Place Mat

1. Warp your loom with the cotton yarn, according to the manufacturer's instructions. Follow the manufacturer's directions for weaving on your loom to make one or more pieces using the T-shirt yarn, sewing the pieces together if necessary to make the desired size place mat.

Any 16- by 12-inch (41 by 30 cm) lap loom such as this one will work for this project.

T-shirt Pillow

Save your favorite childhood shirts with a fun T-shirt pillow. Combine shirts with similar themes to create a fun collection of memories. These two shirts work great on this pillow because you cannot have fries without a Coke.

MATERIALS

> Two printed T-shirts for front
> T-shirt fabric panel for back
> Fusible fleece
> Thread to match fabric
> Scissors
> Rotary cutter, ruler, and mat (optional)
> Fiberfill

INSTRUCTIONS

1. Apply fusible fleece according to the manufacturer's directions onto the back of the two printed shirts you want to use for the front of the pillow.
2. Use a ruler and rotary blade or scissors to cut strips out of the pattern. The size will vary according to your design. Leave an extra 2 inches (5 cm) around the pattern at a minimum. This will allow for the seam and extra visual space. Sew the pieces of fabric together to form the front of your pillow.
3. Cut a piece of fabric for the back of the pillow the same size as the front. Place right sides together. Sew along the outer edge using a $\frac{1}{2}$-inch (1.3 cm) seam allowance. Leave a small opening on one side large enough to add the fiberfill.
4. Once the pieces are sewn together, you need to clip the edges. Make clips in the fabric about $\frac{1}{4}$ inch (0.6 cm) apart along all seams. *Do not* cut too close to the seam lines.
5. Wash separately in a washing machine and then dry. Turn inside out and iron the edges open. Turn the pillow right-side out and carefully use the tip of a chopstick to push the corners of the pillow out.
6. To avoid lumps when stuffing your pillow, use this method: Start with a generous handful of filling. Gently pull the filling loose. The idea is to remove any clumps, while fluffing the fill at the same time. Repeat the process two to three times before inserting the fill into your project. Start stuffing the worked fill into one of the corners farthest from the seam opening. It is best to work your way out. Gently but firmly push the fill into the corner. Pay attention to the outside as you go—you can see any lumps or indents forming. Add filling to the immediate area to smooth out the surface, or remove some filling and "work it" more to remove a stubborn clump. Once the corners are filled, insert small amounts of additional fill.
7. To hand-sew the opening closed, thread the needle with coordinating thread. Keeping your stitches as small as possible, slip-stitch the opening closed. The tiny stitches help to ensure no stuffing will poke out of the hand-sewn seam.

Draft Dodger

Save money on your heating and cooling bills by keeping air from coming under the bottoms of your doors and windows with a pool noodle or pipe insulation and a pair of jeans. This simple project takes an hour or two and can help you save money over the long run. A pipe on either side of the door will slide easily on a smooth surface as the door opens and closes.

MATERIALS

> Straight-leg jeans
> Scissors
> Rotary cutter, ruler, and mat (optional)
> Marker
> Pool noodle or pipe insulation
> Heavy-duty thread
> Jean-A-Ma-Jig
> Sewing machine

INSTRUCTIONS

1. Measure across the bottom of your door and cut two lengths of pool noodle or pipe insulation. Cut the piping 2 inches (1.3 cm) shorter than the door to allow it to open and close fully. Wrap denim around one side and mark on the wrong side of the fabric where you will sew. This is the seam you sew to make a tube for the noodle. It will leave a raw edge, but that will be under the door. Leave enough room for the depth of the door. Repeat for the other side.

2. Fold the fabric over and sew an edge for both sides to form the tubes.

3. Insert a noodle on each side and slide under the door while open. Make any adjustments as needed. You want the noodles to be snug on the inside but loose enough that you can remove the covers for washing.

Tufted Pillow

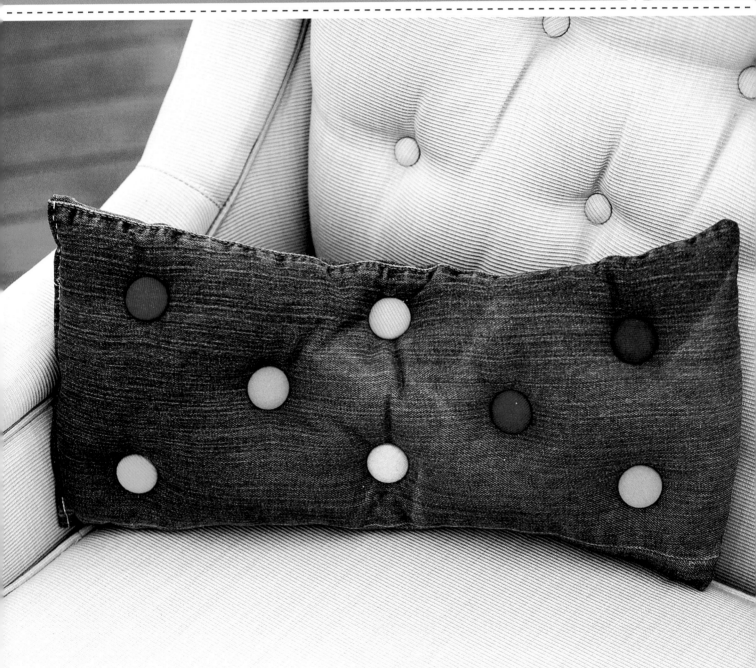

This colorful pillow used T-shirt scraps for covered buttons and a single pant leg. Making a tufted piece is easier than you might think. The cover button kit comes with everything you need to make the fun buttons. I used the covered buttons on the front and back.

MATERIALS

> T-shirt scraps in bold colors
> Denim pant leg
> Scissors
> Thread to match denim fabric
> Fiberfill
> Cover button kit
> Upholstery needle
> Waxed thread
> Sewing machine
> Fabric marker and ruler

INSTRUCTIONS

1. Turn the pant leg inside out. Sew along the bottom seam to close up the leg. Sew on the cut edge and leave a small opening large enough to turn the pillow right-side out and add the fiberfill.

2. Turn the pillow right-side out and carefully use the tip of a chopstick to push the corners of the pillow out.

3. To avoid lumps when stuffing your pillow, use this method: Start with a generous handful of filling. Gently pull the filling loose. The idea is to remove any clumps, while fluffing the fill at the same time. Repeat the process two to three times before inserting the fill into your project. Start stuffing the worked fill into one of the corners farthest from the seam opening. It is best to work your way out. Gently but firmly push the fill into the corner. Pay attention to the outside as you go— you can see any lumps or indents forming. Add filling to the immediate area to smooth out the surface, or remove some filling and "work it" more to remove a stubborn clump. Once the corners are filled, insert small amounts of additional fill. (I made this pillow a little extra fluffy since I knew I would be tufting it.)

4. To hand-sew the opening closed, thread the needle with coordinating thread. Keeping your stitches as small as possible, slip-stitch the opening closed. The tiny stitches help to ensure no stuffing will poke out of the hand-sewn seam.

5. To make the fabric-covered buttons:
   > Place the clear template on the fabric and line up as desired.
   > Trace around the outside of the template with a pencil or pen.
   > Use scissors to cut out the drawn pattern.
   > Center fabric wrong side up over the mold and press the button shell into the mold.
   > Turn the mold over and adjust fabric if needed to re-center.
   > Tuck excess fabric into the button shell.
   > Place a shank-style back over the tucked fabric.
   > Press down firmly with pusher to snap into place.

6. Mark where you would like the buttons to go.

7. Thread the upholstery needle with approximately 18 inches (46 cm) of the waxed upholstery thread. Secure the shank of the first button to the thread using a lark's head knot.

8. Insert the needle (with the button attached) at the first marked tufting point. You are working from the top of the pillow all the way through to the bottom. Firmly push the needle through until it comes out the other side at the same point.

9. Flip the pillow over, pull the thread taut, and slip off the needle. Take another covered button, insert one free end of the thread through the shank of the button, and tie the ends together into a knot. Continue tightening this first knot until the covered button flips down into position and you have created enough tuft. When you have the look you want from both sides, tie a second knot to secure. Trim the ends of the waxed thread so they disappear under the covered button.

10. Sew the other buttons on in the same manner.

Coiled Trivet

love using every scrap I possibly can. This trivet is the perfect example of not letting anything go to waste. I saved the outer seams from leftover projects in a large zip-top bag. Once the bag was overflowing and I could not stuff another piece in, I decided to make something with them. I played around with all sorts of patterns and finally decided on a simple coil.

MATERIALS

> Denim outer seams
> T-shirt or denim fabric for backing
> Heavy-duty scissors
> Straight pins
> Fabric glue

INSTRUCTIONS

1. Using heavy-duty scissors, remove the outer seams from the jeans. Size is not important here.
2. Trim off any excess denim from along the edges of the strip.
3. Add a small dot of fabric glue to an end and wrap the seam around itself. About halfway through, add another small dot of glue and continue wrapping. Once you have reached the end, add an additional dot. Secure in place with a straight pin and allow to dry thoroughly.

4. Once the coils are dry, arrange them into a rectangle or square with the edges of each coil touching one another.
5. Glue the edges of the coils together with small dots of adhesive. Pin in place and allow to dry.
6. Apply a generous amount of glue to the back side of the large shape. Place a piece of denim or T-shirt fabric onto the glue. Once the piece is dry, trim around the edges to remove any excess fabric.

Dazzling Dog Collar

azzling dog collars don't have to be expensive when you make them yourself. All you need is the outside seam from a pair of jeans and a little bit of bling.

MATERIALS

> Denim outer seam
> Heavy-duty scissors
> Sewing machine
> Stud setting tool
> D-ring (optional)
> Jeweled studs or grommets
> Tri-glide (optional)
> Buckle

INSTRUCTIONS

1. Using heavy-duty scissors, remove the outer seam from a pair of jeans.
2. Trim off any excess denim from along the edges of the strip.
3. Measure the length of your dog's neck and add 5 to 7 inches (13 to 18 cm).
4. Sew the open sides of the seam down. Load the seam under the presser foot with the edge close to the needle and sew down the side.
5. There are two ways to secure the ends. You can use a stud or grommet to fasten the ends and secure the buckle as shown in the photos. The second way is to sew them using the following directions and add a D-ring for leash attachment and a tri-glide to allow for length adjustments. You can also use a combination of both.

> To attach the tri-glide, thread one side of the fabric around the middle and pull it through about an inch or two. Stitch down the width of the collar by sewing the loose end back to the collar. Backstitch over the entire stitch to make sure it is secure. Place a second line of stitching closer to the tri-glide for added security.
> Attach the male part of the buckle. String the male part of the buckle through the collar.
> Fold the fabric back through the tri-glide.
> Place the D-ring on the collar and then place the female buckle on the strip.
> Pull the end of the fabric through the buckle about 3 inches (8 cm) and sew the free end back to the collar. Stitch back and forth a few times for extra strength.
> Slide the D-ring against this seam and sew as close to the buckle as you can.
> Sew a third seam a little farther over from the female buckle and push the D-ring against the seam you just created.
> Sew a fourth seam on the other side of the D-ring as close as you can get to the D-ring.
6. Mark along the seam where you want the decorative studs placed.
7. Make a small hole where each stud will go.
8. Set the studs with a stud setting tool following the manufacturer's directions.

Dazzling
Dog Leash

Dazzle is not just for collars. Make a sparkling set with the addition of a leash. This is where extra-long pants come in handy. If one outer seam is not long enough, simply add more to it from the other pant leg.

MATERIALS

> - Denim outer seam
> - Heavy-duty scissors
> - Sewing machine
> - Stud setting tool
> - Swivel hook
> - Jeweled studs
> - Pencil and ruler
> - Stud setting tool

INSTRUCTIONS

1. Using heavy-duty scissors, remove the outer seam from the longest jeans you can find.
2. Trim off any excess denim from along the edges of the strip.
3. Fold the top of the strip over to create a handle and sew securely in place.
4. Fold the other end through the swivel hook and sew it securely in place.
5. Mark along the seam where you want the decorative studs placed. Make a small hole where each stud will go. Set studs using a stud setting tool following the manufacturer's directions.

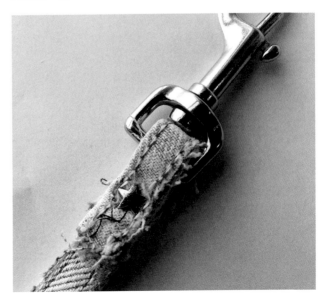

Reversible Contour Burp Cloth

Babies are messy, and reversible burp cloths are a great way to keep both you and them clean. A layer of fleece on the inside of this bib adds an extra layer of protection. You can use patterned or printed T-shirts for more variety or to personalize for a gift.

MATERIALS

> One approximately 19- by 8-inch (48 by 20 cm) piece of denim fabric for the front
> One approximately 19- by 8-inch (48 by 20 cm) piece of T-shirt fabric for the back
> One approximately 19- by 8-inch (48 by 20 cm) piece of fusible fleece
> Sewing machine
> Thread to match fabric
> Straight pins
> Scissors
> Rotary cutter, ruler, and mat (optional)
> Iron and ironing surface

INSTRUCTIONS

1. Follow the manufacturer's directions to adhere the fusible fleece to the wrong side of the T-shirt material.
2. Draw a contour burp cloth pattern or use the one provided on page 74. It is basically a rectangle with a curve along one of the long edges to accommodate mom or baby's neck.
3. Fold your fabric in half and place the pattern along the fold, so you will cut two identical sides at once. Cut around it using your rotary cutter or trace around the pattern and then cut with scissors.
4. Pin the top fabric right-side down onto the right side of the denim. Trim away any excess around the edges.
5. Sew around the edges: Sew ¼ inch (0.6 cm) from the edge almost all the way around, but stop short about 4 inches (10 cm) from where you began. Be sure to backstitch at the beginning and ending stitches.
6. Trim around the edges, especially around the curves, so that the seam edges will lie nicely on the curves once you turn it right-side out. Some people like to notch around the curves. I just trim it in a bit closer.
7. Turn the burp cloth right-side out. Use a chopstick or the end of a wooden spoon to push the curves out.
8. Iron the burp cloth.
9. Topstitch around the edge, sewing ¼ inch (0.6 cm) from the edge. This will close up the opening in the side of the burp cloth as well as finish it decoratively.

Whimsical Coasters

Use up every bit of your scraps and make coasters. There is no right way or wrong way to make these. My squares are approximately 5 inches (13 cm), and I am being generous when I call them squares.

MATERIALS

> Denim scraps
> T-shirt scraps
> Cotton batting or fusible fleece
> Scissors
> Thread to match or contrast
> Iron and ironing surface
> Sewing machine

INSTRUCTIONS

1. Cut two pieces of fabric and one piece of batting all the same size. If you choose to use fusible fleece, follow the manufacturer's directions for use.
2. Make a stack with the right sides of fabric facing out and the batting between.
3. Place a pin in the center.
4. Free-motion stitch around the stack. Do not sew over your pin.

Playful Pincushions

Pincushions are quick and easy to make and are the perfect gift for a new crafter or even a seasoned veteran. I have several in my studio. As my son grows taller, I turn his outgrown and worn-out pants into shorts. I save the legs for crafting. There is always a small stash of legs and random pockets in my fabric bin. You never know when they will come in handy. I used some of those pant legs as the material for these pincushions.

MATERIALS

› Denim pant legs
› Scissors
› Thread
› Straight pins
› Sewing machine
› 20 ounces of fiberfill
› Fairfield Poly-Pellets
› Buttons (saved from sweaters)
› Embroidery floss and needle
› Fabric paint and stencil
› Permanent fabric adhesive

INSTRUCTIONS

1. To make the pincushions, cut open the legs (save the seams for another project).
2. Trace the template and cut it out. Pin to denim and cut out six pieces. I painted on each shape and allowed them to dry before sewing.

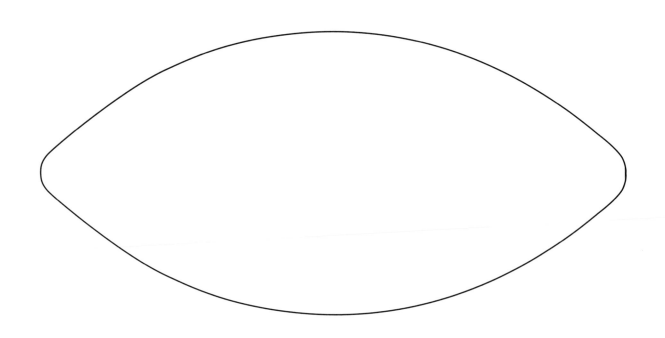

3. Pin the pieces right sides together. Using a ¼-inch (0.6 cm) seam allowance, sew all panels together, leaving a 1-inch (3 cm) opening on one side for turning right-side out. With shape turned right-side out, fill the base with ⅓ cup of weighted filler.

4. Stuff with the fiberfill.

5. Sew closed the open seam with needle and thread.

6. Wrap embroidery floss around the seams to create definition. Tie a knot at the top.

7. Add a dollop of glue to the center, then add a button to cover the thread ends and add a decorative element.

Key Fobs

These key chains are simple, fun, and utilitarian all in one. Use up any small strips and leftover sewing notions to decorate them. These crafty key chains make perfect Valentine's Day, birthday, or Christmas gifts for your girlfriends and guy friends. I made five in about an hour.

MATERIALS

> Denim scraps
> Ribbon
> Buttons, studs, or other embellishments
> Scissors
> Glue stick
> Sewing machine and thread
> Key fob hardware
> Pliers
> Ruler or tape measure (optional)

INSTRUCTIONS

1. Cut the denim to desired length, approximately 1 by 10 inches (3 by 25 cm). You can make them larger or smaller to fit your needs. Just make sure you have the right size hardware to fit the width of the fabric strip.
2. Hand-sew the buttons or attach the studs on the right side of the denim strip. If you are using ricrac, use a glue stick to hold it in place on the outside of the strip. Then sew in place. If you are placing ribbon down the center, sew along the edges on both sides of the ribbon and trim off any loose fibers.
3. Fold the strip in half, wrong sides together, and follow the packaging directions to affix the key fob hardware.
4. Attach the key ring to the rectangular piece.

Stitch and Slash
Pin Tuck T-shirt Purse

combined pin tucks with the Stitch and Slash technique to create a lot of flow and movement in this purse. I like the rough rustic look, so I left my edges raw and threads hanging. I find beauty in imperfection. The bag also has a rough liner where you can see the inner stitches. The straps were created from a thrift store belt. I recommend making a braided strap or a simple fabric strap as an alternative. The dangle I added was also found at the thrift store. I like fun fashion on the cheap.

MATERIALS

> Four 12- by 24-inch (30 by 61 cm) pieces of T-shirt material in different colors
> One 12- by 24-inch (30 by 61 cm) piece of cotton for the liner
> One 12- by 24-inch (30 by 61 cm) piece of fusible fleece
> Two 4- by 12-inch (10 by 30 cm) pieces of T-shirt material and fusible fleece for side panels
> Metal ring belt and strip of T-shirt material for the strap
> Dangle for a decorative accent (optional)
> Marking tool
> Scissors
> Rotary cutter, ruler, and mat (optional)
> Straight pins
> Sewing machine and thread
> Iron and ironing surface

INSTRUCTIONS

1. I fused the bottom layer to fusible fleece for extra stability and to give the purse shape. On the back side I fused a single layer of cotton fabric to use as a liner.

2. Starting from the left selvedge edge and using a removable marking tool and ruler, mark lines for the fabric pin tucks. The first marking is 1 inch (3 cm) from the left edge. Space the remaining marks 1 inch (3 cm) apart. Sew along the marked lines.

3. Place scissors inside three of the four layers, cutting evenly in between the sewn lines (see photo).

4. Using the ruler and cutting mat, square the piece.
5. Starting from the center point, topstitch across the width of the fabric, securing the pin tucks. Measure over 3 inches (8 cm) and sew again. Continue measuring and stitching rows of pin tucks. Using the ruler and cutting mat, square up the ends of the fabric panel that you will be turning into the purse. Press pin tucks in the opposite direction and stitch between the previously stitched sections to secure pin tucks.

6. To form the purse, sew the edges to the side panels using a ¹/₂-inch (1.3 cm) seam allowance with the

raw edges sticking out. I added the strapping by sewing on simple loops to the inside and attaching the metal rings to the loops.

Painted Mobile

Have a three-seasons room that needs a little movement or a baby that needs visual stimulation? Try a simple mobile made from scrap denim and painted in contrasting colors with simple patterns.

MATERIALS

> ⟩ Denim scraps
> ⟩ Wooden embroidery hoop
> ⟩ Twine
> ⟩ Metal beads
> ⟩ Americana acrylic paint in white and coral blush and paintbrush
> ⟩ Scissors
> ⟩ Thread
> ⟩ Straight pins
> ⟩ Sewing machine with thread
> ⟩ Fiberfill

INSTRUCTIONS

1. Make eleven to thirteen hearts by placing two pieces of denim together with wrong sides facing and cutting heart shapes out of the pieces. Pin them together in the center.
2. Once all the hearts are cut and pinned together, sew around the edges using a ¼-inch (0.6 cm) seam allowance, leaving a small opening for the fiberfill.
3. Stuff each heart. Sew the opening closed and repeat for each heart.
4. On a covered work surface, paint random designs on one side of the hearts. Once the hearts are dry, flip them over and paint the other side. Allow to dry.
5. Cut a thin strip of denim to wrap around the wooden embroidery hoop. Secure the end with a dollop of glue or tuck inside a loop.
6. Add the hearts to strands of twine by sewing them in place at the top and bottom of the heart. Repeat and place the hearts randomly yet spaced equally apart on the strings. Tie to the top of the hoop.

7. Tie three strands of twine to the hoop to form a hanger. Add the metal beads at the bottom of the strands of hearts and add a few hanging down from the hoop as accents.

Baskets

For me, upcycling is a way of life and a step to making a smaller impact on the earth. My friends and family like to give me their worn-out clothes to use in my crafting and sewing. These particular baskets are from the overalls of a friend's father. When he passed away, her mom asked if I could use any of his clothes for crafting. I would never turn down good denim because of its versatility, and I would normally make memory pillows out of shirts in lieu of flowers. The memory pillows have become a tradition of mine. Instead of taking the overalls apart and adding them to my denim pile, I decided to create something a little different and make her a set of baskets for everyday use—a small way to keep him around and close. Her home decor is simple with accents of earth tones. The fabric I found was the perfect blend of the two, and I also knew she loves nature and birds. The embellishments and trims for each basket are pieces I found in my stash that I thought would make the baskets prettier. I even used little twigs as an accent. You do not have to spend a lot of money to make things pretty, and it is always nice to bring a bit of the outside in.

I wanted the baskets to have some structure and stiffness and not flop over. I used Structure interfacing, which comes with fusible webbing on the back, saving an entire sewing step, and it gave the baskets a nice sturdy feel. Ironing the interlining to the denim also gave it a nice crisp feel while retaining the soft worn-in look.

It takes about two hours to make all three baskets and is a beginner-to-intermediate project.

MEASUREMENTS

You may need to alter the measurements to utilize the jeans that you are using. Add 1/2 inch (1.3 cm) to the width of the lining for the seam allowance.

Small basket: 7 1/2 by 8 inches (19 by 20 cm) with a 2-inch (5 cm) box corner

Medium basket: 7 1/2 by 8 1/2 inches (19 by 22 cm) with a 1 3/4-inch (4.4 cm) box corner

Large basket: 7 1/2 by 9 inches (19 by 23 cm) with a 1 1/2-inch (3.8 cm) box corner

MATERIALS

- › Jeans or overalls
- › Fabric for lining (add 3 inches [7.6 cm] to jean measurement for lining fabric and interfacing)
- › Fairfield Structure interfacing (to give body and structure)
- › Iron and ironing surface

- › Sewing machine with denim needle and thread
- › Scissors
- › Straight pins
- › Pencil
- › Ruler
- › Needle and thread
- › Doilies, buttons, and other embellishments

INSTRUCTIONS

1. Choose a section of the leg of the jeans where the top and bottom of your cut piece are the same width. Using the dimensions above, measure and cut pieces, one for each basket. You can adjust the sizes as needed.

2. Iron interfacing to the wrong side of lining fabric.

3. Sew the bottom seam, leaving a gap of 3 inches (8 cm) in the middle. Press all the seams open.

4. Measure 2 inches (5 cm) from the corner seam in both directions and on both sides of the fabric.

5. Pull out the sides of your bag. Place one seam on top of the other seam. Put your pin through the top mark. Make sure the seams are open to reduce bulk.

6. Remove the pin and hold the fabric in place. With a ruler, draw a line across the fabric and sew along that line. This will make your box pleat.

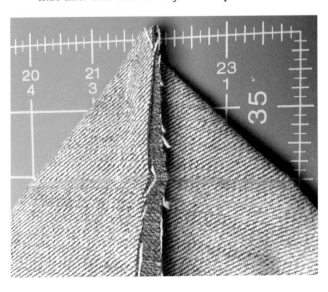

7. For the outside of the baskets, turn the jeans wrong side out and sew the bottom seam. Then press the seam open.

8. Measure 2 inches (5 cm) from each side edge of the fabric. The front and back of the jeans may be different widths, so the seam may not be on the edge.

9. Make the box corners.

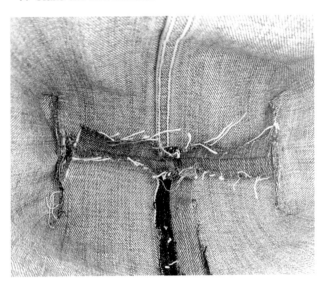

10. Turn the bag right-side out and gently pull the right side of the bag out through the lining. Hand-stitch or machine topstitch the gap in the lining. Push the lining back into the bag and iron the top edge of the bag.

11. Add any decorative elements to each bag.

TIP: If necessary, turn the machine by hand over bulky seams.

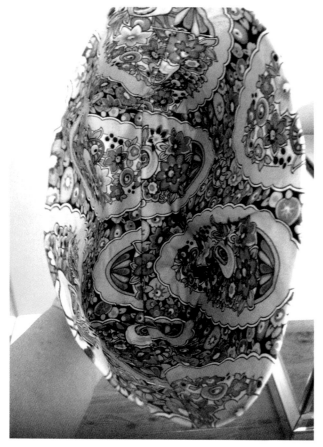

The inside of the basket.

The lining ready for the denim part to be attached.

The bottom of the basket.

The basket with inner lining and outer basket held together.

Fabric Flower

Fabric flowers can be fun embellishments on a variety of projects, and are another great way to use fabric scraps.

MATERIALS

> Fabric
> Scissors
> Thread in two colors
> Needle and thread or sewing machine
> Button

INSTRUCTIONS

1. Cut a piece of fabric about 1 by 10 inches (3 by 25 cm). Fold the strip of fabric in half lengthways with right sides together.

2. Thread the machine with different color thread in the bobbin and in the top (I used black and white threads). Sew together the long edge with a ¼-inch (0.6 cm) seam allowance, without backstitching at each end. You can do this by hand or by machine. If you use a machine, set it to the longest stitch length.

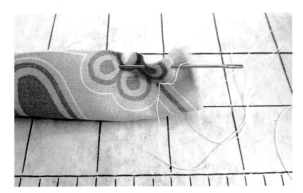

3. Use a safety pin to turn the tube right-side out.

4. Locate the loose thread ends of the seam and knot them together at one end of the tube. At the other end, pull one of the threads to evenly gather up the tube. Pull up about 5 inches (13 cm) of thread and place the length onto a sewing needle, ready to sew up the flower.

5. Glue a button over the center of the flower.

TIP: If you need more gathers, pull on one of the threads at the knotted end. The different colors of thread will make this easier—you can choose which color is the gathering thread at both ends.

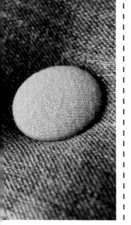

Alphabet
Bean Bags

My daughter attends a Montessori school, and the preschool teacher asked for ideas on tactile or interactive alphabets. That is how the alphabet bean bags came to fruition. The children can run their fingers over the iron-on appliqués, and they can spell words and play games with them, too. Best of all, they can be washed when they get dirty. The filling for the bags is a combination of fiberfill and Poly-Pellets. The pellets give the bags weight so they can be used in a toss game. There are letters on both sides of the bags, for more spelling options.

MATERIALS

> One hundred 4-inch (10 cm) denim squares
> Fiberfill
> Fairfield Poly-Pellets
> Iron-on letters
> Sizzix Big Shot Pro or Sizzix Big Shot and 4-inch square die-cut (optional)
> Scissors
> Rotary cutter, ruler, and mat (optional but recommended)
> Iron and ironing surface
> Thread
> Straight pins
> Sewing machine with thread

INSTRUCTIONS

1. Cut out one hundred squares of denim. I used my Big Shot and a die-cut for this project. It is a fast way to cut out multiples of the same object. If you don't have access to one, you can use a ruler, rotary cutter, and cutting mat.

2. On a safe ironing surface, follow the manufacturer's directions to affix iron-on letters to the right side of the denim. Each package of letters contains approximately forty-six letters. I left a few squares blank so they could be used as spacers when making multiple words.

3. Place two squares with wrong sides together on the sewing machine and sew around the edges using a 1/4-inch (0.6 cm) seam allowance, leaving a small opening for the Poly-Pellets and fiberfill. Repeat for all the pre-cut squares.

4. Add a tablespoon or two of the Poly-Pellets to the opening, and then add the fiberfill. Pin the opening closed. Keep the piece pinned closed until the piece is under the presser foot, then remove the pin. The pellets will come out if it is not pinned closed.

Denim Place Mats

The denim place mats go with the hammock cover and director's chair as part of our camping gear. The denim is perfect for camping because it is durable and washable. You could also use the place mats as your everyday table mats. Large rectangular place mats approximately 12 by 18 inches (30 by 46 cm) or 14 by 20 inches (36 by 51 cm) will hold an entire place setting. Use whichever size works best for the amount of denim you have or the size of your table.

MATERIALS

> Denim fabric
> Jean pockets
> Scissors
> Rotary cutter, ruler, and mat (optional)
> Jean-A-Ma-Jig
> Iron and ironing surface
> Denim thread
> Straight pins
> Sewing machine with denim needle and denim thread

INSTRUCTIONS

1. Cut the denim to 12 by 18 inches (30 by 46 cm) or 14 by 20 inches (36 by 51 cm). Sew a straight line along the edges using a $\frac{1}{2}$-inch (1.3 cm) seam allowance so that when you wash the place mat the denim does not fray further than desired. The gold denim thread looks really great for this and gives a designer touch.

2. Wash the place mat to create the fray on the edge. Iron the place mat before sewing on the pocket.

3. If you have deconstructed jeans previously for other projects and have pockets saved, use a variety of pocket styles for a whimsical touch. If you need to deconstruct for the pockets, cut the legs off the jeans below the pocket. Then, with your scissors as close to the edge of the pocket as possible, trim along the edge, going all the way around the pocket.

4. Attach the pocket to the place mat. Sew along the stitching of the pocket to hide the new stitches. The Jean-A-Ma-Jig comes in handy when attaching the pockets, as the denim can be difficult to get started. If necessary, turn the machine by hand over bulky seams.

Mug Wrap

This easy-sew mug wrap is a perfect gift for the coffee or cocoa lover. I created the design on the denim by trying out the fancy stitches on my sewing machine. If your machine does not have fancy stitches, you can freestyle your own design.

MATERIALS

- › Denim fabric
- › Fusible fleece
- › Scissors
- › Rotary cutter, ruler, and mat (optional)
- › Button
- › 4 inches (10 cm) elastic, ¼-inch (0.6 cm) wide
- › Straight pins
- › Sewing machine with thread

INSTRUCTIONS

1. Cut one of each of the following pieces:
   - › 5- by 11-inch (13 by 28 cm) front fabric (denim)
   - › 5- by 11-inch (13 by 28 cm) backing fabric
   - › 5- by 11-inch (13 by 28 cm) fusible fleece
2. Stitch the design of your choice on the front of the denim.
3. Iron the fusible fleece onto the wrong side of the backing fabric. Lay front and back fabric pieces right sides together.
4. To form the elastic loop, fold elastic in half and slide the looped side between the two pieces of fabric. Center it along the short side and pin elastic in place. Pin both layers of fabric together.
5. Sew around the two layers of fabric using a ¼-inch (0.6 cm) seam allowance. Leave a 2-inch (5 cm) gap on one side to turn the piece right-side out.
6. Turn right-side out and iron flat. Pin the opening closed and topstitch around the mug wrap with a ⅛-inch (0.3 cm) seam allowance.
7. To affix the button on the mug wrap, fold the edge with the elastic ½ inch (1.3 cm) over the non-elastic edge. Using a pencil, mark the edge of the elastic on the mug wrap. Sew the button onto the mark.

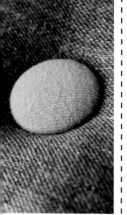

Art Apron

Make an art apron for all of your crafty endeavors. Not only can you craft in style, but you can say you made it, too. Use smaller jeans if you want to make a child-size apron. This particular apron was styled for a friend who loves pink. You can give your apron any theme or color scheme.

MATERIALS

> Denim jeans
> Jean pocket
> Waistband for strap
> Rotary cutter, ruler, and mat (optional)
> Jean-A-Ma-Jig
> Ribbon and trim
> Fabric or denim for the tie
> Button
> Stencil, fabric paint, and/or other trim or embellishments
> Iron and ironing surface
> Scissors
> Denim thread
> Straight pins
> Sewing machine with denim needle and denim thread

INSTRUCTIONS

1. Cut off a leg right underneath the pocket.
2. Cut out the back pocket entirely, getting as close to the seam edge as possible, or use a pocket from your stash. Hopefully you have a nice stash of denim by now.
3. Turn the pant leg over so the front is down. Cut the pant leg open by cutting along the outer seam.
4. Fold the piece right sides together and cut out a crescent shape at the widest part. This will give the curve at the bottom of the apron.
5. Sew around the entire piece using a 1/2-inch (1.3 cm) seam allowance. I used a contrasting thread for a decorative punch.
6. Pin the pocket into position and sew into place. The Jean-A-Ma-Jig comes in handy here.
7. Measure the desired length around the neck and cut the waistband, keeping the buttonhole end for attachment. Sew on the waistband at one of the top edges of the apron. Find a button that fits the opening and sew it onto the apron by hand.
8. Cut a strip of denim or fabric to create the ties at the waist. Attach evenly on both sides.
9. Sew on the embellishments as desired. I made fabric rosettes for the strap. See page 100 for instructions.
10. I used stencils and paint to add even more details. Use fabric paint so that it does not wash off easily.

Rosette

MATERIALS

> › One strip of fabric or ribbon
> › Needle and thread
> › Thimble
> › Button

INSTRUCTIONS

1. I like to start with a fabric strip that is approximately 1½ inch (2.6 cm) wide and 18 inches (46 cm) long. Fold the fabric strip in half lengthwise and round off the corners with shears. You can vary the size and look of your rosette by using different widths and lengths of fabric.

2. Cut a piece of thread that is several inches longer than the length of the fabric strip. Run a line of long stitches along the raw inner edge of the folded strip. Tightly gather the strip by pulling on the needle-end of the thread. You can also do this step by adjusting the straight stitch on your sewing machine to the longest possible stitch.

3. Roll the fabric strip into a rosette. Begin at one end, and as you roll the fabric, stab-stitch through the back portion of the flower with a needle and thread to keep its shape. Use a thimble to get through multiple layers of fabric.

4. Tie a knot on the underside of the rosette.

5. Embellish the rosette as you wish. I chose a button, which can be glued on or sewn on by hand.

There are three different edging techniques for the memory pillows shown in the photograph. Try one or try them all to create a unique trio of pillows. The size and shape of your pillows will depend on the size of the image on the shirt.

Cut Edge (Blue) Pillow

MATERIALS

> T-shirt
> Scissors
> Rotary cutter, ruler, and mat (optional but recommended)
> Fiberfill
> Straight pins
> Sewing machine with thread

INSTRUCTIONS

1. Cut the design from the front of the T-shirt. Leave as much room around the image as is possible while still cutting straight lines. The ruler and rotary cutter work well for this.

2. Cut a piece of fabric for the back of the pillow the same size as the front. Place pieces wrong sides together. Sew along the outer edge, allowing as much fabric as desired for the fringe you will cut. I chose a contrasting thread for additional detail. Leave a small opening on one side large enough to add the fiberfill.

3. Once the pieces are sewn together, you need to clip the edges. Make clips in the fabric about 1 inch (3 cm) apart along all seams. *Do not* cut too close to the seam lines. You can leave the fringe loose or you can tie it in small knots.

4. To avoid lumps when stuffing your pillow, use this method: Start with a generous handful of filling. Gently pull the filling loose. The idea is to remove any clumps, while fluffing the fill at the same time. Repeat the process two to three times before inserting the fill into your project. Start stuffing the worked fill into one of the corners farthest from the seam opening. It is best to work your way out. Gently but firmly push the fill into the corner. Pay attention to the outside as you go—you can see any lumps or indents forming. Add filling to the immediate area to smooth out the surface, or remove some filling and "work it" more to remove a stubborn clump. Once the corners are filled, insert small amounts of additional fill.

5. Machine- or hand-sew the opening closed.

Faux Braided Edge (Orange) Pillow

The best part of making this pillow is that there is no sewing involved, and you get a fun braided look on the edge. This pillow uses a pre-made pillow form. Once you cut out your T-shirt pieces, measure them and choose a form that is 2 inches (5 cm) smaller all the way around than your fabric. This allows for the "poof" of the pillow.

MATERIALS

> T-shirt
> Scissors
> Rotary cutter, ruler, and mat (optional but recommended)
> 10-inch pillow form
> Straight pins
> Paper clip or crochet hook

INSTRUCTIONS

1. To make a round shape, I centered a large platter on the T-shirt and cut around it. I am good with a rotary cutter and used it to cut the fabric. If you are not, trace around the image and use a pair of scissors.

2. Cut a piece of fabric for the back of the pillow the same size as the front.

3. Cut fringe all around that is 1 inch (3 cm) wide and 2 inches (5 cm) deep. I used the inch markings on my cutting mat, but if you don't have one, you can estimate. The fringe doesn't need to be perfect. It is best to cut both layers together, so that the fringe on the front and back of the pillow match.

4. Cut a small slit in the center of each piece of fringe, about 1/4 inch (0.6 cm) long. Make sure it's not too close to the end, or it may rip through. About 1/2 inch (1.3 cm) from the end should be good.

5. Insert pillow form.

6. Use a large crochet hook or unbend a paper clip to use as a hook. Choose one of the pieces of fringe in the middle of the bottom piece. Working from the bottom, stick the paper clip through the slit and catch the matching piece of fringe from the top piece. Pull the bottom fringe through the top. Put the paper clip through the bottom fringe piece that you just pulled through the first top fringe piece, and catch the top fringe piece to the left of the first one. Pull it through and continue pulling fringe through each piece, alternating each time between the top and bottom, continuing around the corners.

7. When you get to the last piece of fringe, cut it in half through the slit to get two narrower pieces of fringe. Use these to tie a double knot around the piece of fringe you started with; tuck the knot inside the pillow.

Tied Edges (Green) Pillow

Not only does this T-shirt pillow bring back memories from summer tennis, but it also incorporates the tiny black rubber bands my son wore on his braces. Create your memory pillow and add little details that are important to the recipient. You could add prize ribbons, pins, buttons, and other memorabilia.

MATERIALS

> T-shirt
> Scissors
> Rotary cutter, ruler, and mat (optional but recommended)
> Fiberfill
> Straight pins
> Sewing machine or needle with coordinating thread
> Small rubber bands

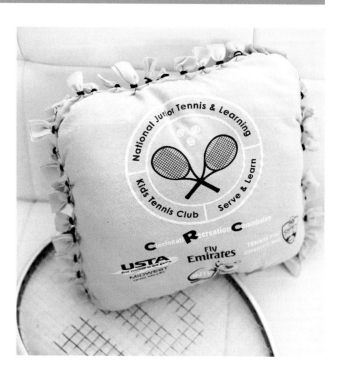

INSTRUCTIONS

1. When cutting the design out of the front of the T-shirt, leave as much room around the image as is possible while still cutting straight lines. The ruler and rotary cutter work well for this.
2. Cut a piece of fabric for the back of the pillow the same size as the front. Place wrong sides together. Sew along the outer edge using a $1/2$- to 1-inch (1.3 to 5 cm) seam allowance using a coordinating thread. Leave a small opening on one side large enough to add the fiberfill. (You can adjust the size of the fringe according to the size of your finished pillow.)
3. Once the pieces are sewn together, you need to clip the edges. Make clips in the fabric about $1/4$ inch (0.6 cm) apart along all seams. *Do not* cut too close to the seam lines. Wrap the rubber bands around each set of fringed pieces.
4. To avoid lumps when stuffing your pillow, use this method: Start with a generous handful of filling. Gently pull the filling loose. The idea is to remove any clumps, while fluffing the fill at the same time. Repeat the process two to three times before inserting the fill into your project. Start stuffing the worked fill into one of the corners farthest

from the seam opening. It is best to work your way out. Gently but firmly push the fill into the corner. Pay attention to the outside as you go—you can see any lumps or indents forming. Add filling to the immediate area to smooth out the surface, or remove some filling and "work it" more to remove a stubborn clump. Once the corners are filled, insert small amounts of additional fill.

5. Machine- or hand-sew the opening closed.

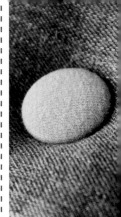

Christmas Tags

These tag-shaped Christmas ornaments are fun to add to your holiday packaging, tie around a bottle of wine, or use to decorate the Christmas tree. If you want to use the denim tags for your luggage, you can change the motif of the stencil. The tags would also make a fun garland or banner that you can use to decorate a mantel or special space. For this project I used double-sided Stiffen. It gives the piece a little structure and stability. If you cannot find Stiffen, I would use a double-sided fusible adhesive.

MATERIALS

> Denim scraps
> Scissors
> Rotary cutter, ruler, and mat (optional)
> Pencil or pen
> Shipping tag for tracing
> Ribbon and ribbon hanger
> Fairfield Stiffen interfacing
> Straight pins
> Sewing machine with thread
> Fabric paint
> Stencil and stencil brush
> Iron and ironing surface
> Miscellaneous buttons and flowers
> Glue gun and glue sticks

INSTRUCTIONS

1. Using either a large denim piece or a bunch of smaller scraps, adhere the double-sided Stiffen on the wrong side of the denim using an iron on a covered work surface.

2. Draw or trace the tag shape on the interfacing and, using heavy-duty scissors, cut the tag shape out. You can fuse the back side layer of denim before or after this step. I prefer to do it after so the pieces are easier to cut out, and I also like to place the ribbon hanger between the layers before fusing. If you fuse first, you can use glue or staples to adhere the ribbon.

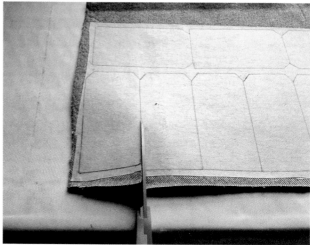

4. Once the paint is dry, you can add embellishments to the top and it's ready to hang.

3. Use a variety of stencils to add details to the denim. I like to let the stenciled image run off the edges sometimes. When stenciling on fabric, less paint is best. Add multiple layers of paint to develop a darker solid surface. Avoid loading the brush with too much paint; overloading causes the paint to bleed through the stencil.

Denim Star Ornaments

The denim star ornaments are a fun project to do with children. The snowman and tree are simple items to paint, and children love to help, especially when it comes to painting. I let my children use the Sizzix die-cut machine. Adult supervision is suggested for younger children or beginners. I also closely supervise older children with ironing.

MATERIALS

- Sizzix Big Shot Pro or Sizzix Big Shot and star die-cut, item #A10181, or star template for tracing
- Scissors
- Rotary cutter, ruler, and mat (optional but recommended)
- Fairfield Stiffen interfacing
- Straight pins
- Sewing machine with thread
- Acrylic paint or fabric paint
- Small paintbrushes
- Iron and ironing surface
- Miscellaneous buttons and flowers

INSTRUCTIONS

1. Using either a large denim piece or a bunch of smaller scraps, adhere the double-sided Stiffen on the wrong side of the denim using an iron on a covered work surface and adding ribbon hangers between the layers, if desired. Repeat for the back side, too.
2. Use scissors or the rotary cutter and mat to cut the fabric down to size. I use a ruler to measure, too. Place the layered fabric in the die-cut machine. Follow the manufacturer's directions for best results. You can also choose to cut the stars first and fuse them individually, as shown in the photos.

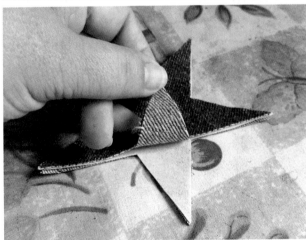

3. Remove the excess fabric and star. Repeat for as many stars as you need.
4. Paint any images you would like on the ornaments. We chose snowmen and trees as our theme last Christmas for our packaging and handmade cards.

Braided
Animal Toy

This braid technique sounds more complicated than it is. I learned to do the two-strand crown sinnet (aka box braid or square braid) at summer camp when I was seven. Once you get the rhythm, it goes very fast. If you have a big dog, make the strips longer and wider. If you have a cat or small dog, you can make the strips skinnier. The nice thing about this toy is you can wash it when it gets dirty and stinky.

MATERIALS

> Two 36- by 1-inch (91 by 3 cm) strips of denim (you can adjust this size)
> Pen or pencil
> Scissors

INSTRUCTIONS

1. Cross the two denim strips to form an X.

2. Fold the top left strip across the bottom left strip and the bottom right strip across the top right strip.

3. Pull the bottom strip over the first horizontal strip and under the second on both sides. Pull firmly on the strips to tighten the knot.

4. Repeat until you have the desired length for your dog or cat toy.

5. Tie a double knot at the end to finish. You can add an extra stitch by hand to secure the strips, but don't use glue as it is not safe for pets.

TIPS: Keep your knots consistent. When tightening, pull two strips to one side, two to the other. Tighten all four strips firmly.

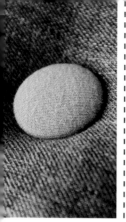

Denim Slipcover

Making a slipcover for a piece of furniture takes more time than skill. If you take the time to get the measurements correct, your piece will fit. This was a really old ottoman that a friend was ready to pitch. I saved it because it was still sturdy and we needed something for the kids to use in the basement. The original piece had torn fabric and was a little more used on one side than the other. I covered the piece with Poly-Fil Project Fleece to smooth out the surface and give a nice solid base. For the skirting I happened to have a denim skirt. I used it, pockets and all.

MATERIALS

› Denim fabric in various sizes and colors
› Staple gun and staples
› Poly-Fil Project Fleece
› Rotary cutter, ruler, and mat
› Jean-A-Ma-Jig
› Iron and ironing surface
› Scissors
› Straight pins
› Sewing machine with denim needle and denim thread

The stool prior to covering.

INSTRUCTIONS

1. Remove any skirting or excess material. Once excess material is removed, cover the piece with Poly-Fil Project Fleece and secure in place with a staple gun.
2. Measure the piece for two pieces of fabric: a top and the skirting. Add an inch to all your measurements—you can always trim off the excess. I used horizontal stripes for the top piece and vertical stripes for the skirting.
3. The top piece of fabric is made by sewing denim pieces in contrasting colors right sides together. Make sure to iron the seams open and flat for best fit. If you'd prefer raw edges, sew the pieces wrong sides together.
4. For the skirting, I used fabric pieces with a hem already in place. You can choose to sew a hem by folding the fabric up and sewing in place, or you can use a raw edge and sew around the bottom edge to prevent excessive fraying when washed.
5. Sew your fabric strips to make the two fabric pieces the size of your measurements. I used raw edges on the skirting seams.
6. After you have sewn the denim fabric pieces to the size of your measurements, place the pieces in position on the footstool and adjust if needed. Once you have the fabric in the correct size and position, pin the pieces together with right sides facing. (For raw edges, sew the pieces wrong sides together.)
7. Be sure to use heavy-duty thread, as you want this piece to be durable. Sew the pieces together. Do another test fit for the cover. Make any adjustments. When you are satisfied, add an additional stitch for extra durability, trim the excess, and iron open any seams.

Visual Index

Pencil or Make-up Case
8

Baby Bibs
18

Sailor Tote
10

Tote for Kids
20

Planter Pincushion
13

Pretty Patterned Headband
22

Chevron Handbag
15

Stitch and Slash Pillow
25

About the Author

Growing up in a small midwestern town, Niki Meiners was surrounded by a modest, resourceful, and very entrepreneurial family. Her simple upbringing spurred her "can-do" attitude and gave her the confidence to try any challenge placed before her. She knew there was more out there than just her small town, and so she set off after high school to explore the world. It was through these travels that she discovered her love of art and her desire to make the world a prettier place. It was not until she suffered a paralyzing illness, transverse myelitis, that she realized she wanted to reconsider her corporate career as Chief Paper Pusher, and her thoughts immediately turned to her first passion, art. In 2003 she began an odyssey that would take her from product design to publication and everywhere in between. She is known for her distinctive, high-quality creations that feature a diverse mix of styles and highly creative approach to even the smallest detail. Niki is an "idea architect," easily outlining every project from concept to completion. Her creations are simultaneously beautiful and functional and have been featured in the industry's leading craft and lifestyle publications and manufacturers' websites.